MID-CHESHIRE
MEMORIES

MID-CHESHIRE MEMORIES

VOLUME 1: The Horseman and his Family;
The Apprentice Mechanic's Tale; The Apprentice Fitter's Tale;
The Fireman's Tale of the End of Steam

**Elizabeth Ellen Osborne, Geoffrey Mellor
Peter Buckley and Bruce Fisher**

ISBN 1 901253 28 7

First published March 2002

Published in Gt Britain by:
Léonie Press
an imprint of Anne Loader Publications
13 Vale Road, Hartford
Northwich, Cheshire CW8 1PL
Tel: 01606 75660   Fax: 01606 77609
E-mail: anne@aloaderpubs.u-net.com
Websites: www.leoniepress.com
www.aloaderpubs.u-net.com

Book: Edited, typeset and printed by:
Anne Loader Publications

Acknowledgements and thanks to J R Lee for photograph used on front cover and title page

About the authors

Elizabeth Ellen Osborne was born at Shipbrook, near Northwich, Cheshire, in 1914. Her father was an agricultural worker and the family lived in a tied cottage. When she left school at 14 she went to work as a 'between maid' at the local Rectory. Two years later she became a kitchen maid and after various other posts was employed as a lady's companion.

Following her marriage she was a nurse, a 'dinner lady' and a much-loved foster mother. As a Royal British Legion welfare officer she rode round Mid-Cheshire on a 90cc motorcycle until she was 80 years old.

She has a phenomenal photo-graphic memory and her vivid recollections paint a fascinating picture of her early family life. Her book "Nellie's Story", pub-lished in April 2000, has been a great success.

Geoffrey Mellor was born in 1934 and moved to 'Bottom Lostock', Northwich with his family when he was four. He went to Rudheath Secondary School for Boys and after a short spell at ICI, worked in the motor trade locally for Mr Harry Breeze and J W Foster and Sons before signing up as a 'regular' to join The Royal Engineers in August 1952.

He and his wife Evelyn have been married 39 years. They live in Winsford and have four daughters, Tracey, Audrey, Stella and Rachel; the three oldest are married and Rachel is due to wed in July 2002. Geoff and Evelyn have two grand-daughters and four grandsons.

Geoff is now retired. His interests include golf and Shire Horses. Friends know him as an avid teller of anecdotes and jokes.

About the authors (cont)

Peter Buckley was born in Northwich in April 1938. He says: "I was educated (almost) at Timber Lane School, Victoria Road School and Rudheath Secondary School for Boys.

"I trained as a fitter/turner at W.J. Yarwood's shipyard, returning there for a short while after National Service in The Royal Corps of Signals in Singapore.

"I drifted into the plastics industry where I worked until taking early retirement.

"I'm married to Freda, and we have two sons and one granddaughter.

"Among my interests are reading, music, watercolour painting and struggling to learn to use computers."

Bruce Fisher and his family moved to Cheshire from East London in the 1960s. After starting as an engine cleaner he later became a fireman working on heavy freight as well as passenger and express parcel trains.

When Northwich loco depot was 'dieselised' he left the railway and joined the RAF where he trained as a transport driver, serving in Uxbridge, driving coaches and ambulances carrying emergency aero-medical evacuees. He was also posted to Libya for the British withdrawal following the country's revolution.

After the RAF he entered the demolition industry and for 18 years ran his own demolition and haulage company, specialising in reclaiming bricks for resale in London. Then he moved back to Northwich and became a site manager for a large demolition company. Deciding to take a break from demolition work he is now with a local bus company.

Preface

The last century has seen more change than any other in history and we at the Mid-Cheshire-based Léonie Press believe that the memories of those who lived during this period should be collected for posterity before it is too late.

This book is the first of what we hope will be a series covering ways of life and occupations that have now changed out of all recognition or vanished for ever. It was inspired by "Footsteps in History – An Oral History Project for the Millennium" which included an essay competition that I was asked to judge.

The project involved the Mid-Cheshire College and the Salt Museum in conjunction with Winsford Willow Wood, Darnhall County Primary and Northwich Witton Church Walk Schools coming together to collect and record local history. The children interviewed their grandparents to discover a world long gone. These oral accounts were recorded and used as an inspiration for projects within the schools and the college. An exhibition bringing together the oral accounts and the artwork, entitled "Footsteps in History", was held at the Salt Museum, Northwich on November 14, 2000 and was opened by the Cheshire author, Alan Garner.

Entrants in the essay competition were asked to write up to 800 words describing an aspect of the changing landscape in this area that they could remember but many others might have forgotten. If this happened to include walking or trains, all the better, said the organisers. The competition was open to anyone over 18 years of age whose work had not previously appeared in print. The winning entry was published in the *Northwich Guardian*.

After choosing the winner, I decided that it would be a great shame if the other contributions were simply lost to posterity, so Léonie Press published them all in a booklet which was available as part of the "Footsteps in History" exhibition. We asked the authors if they would like to elaborate on their short essays and gave them free rein. Thus were Peter Buckley and Bruce Fisher's contributions to "Mid-Cheshire Memories" conceived, as they respectively recalled their time working at one of Northwich's long-gone shipyards and as a fireman on steam locomotives.

Geoffrey Mellor then approached Léonie Press with his account of his childhood and years as an apprentice mechanic, and this immediately seemed to gell with the other two writers' memories.

Finally, Elizabeth Ellen ("Nellie") Osborne had achieved significant local success with her book "Nellie's Story: A Life of Service" published by Léonie Press in April 2000 and her fans clamoured for more. She subsequently wrote a postscript to the book, looking again at her rural childhood and concentrating on her father's life as a horseman on local farms. This seemed to fit naturally with the other authors' accounts of men's jobs which had altered significantly or virtually disappeared.

In this way **"Mid-Cheshire Memories: Volume One"** was born. We have published the four memoirs in chronological order. We hope that readers will enjoy the book and that other local people will be inspired to write their own contributions to subsequent volumes.

Léonie Press is committed to capturing the recollections of "ordinary" folk who lived in the Vale Royal area and shaped its history during the last 150 years – when there have been incredible changes and developments in technology, agriculture, transport, health and family life.

Help us to keep those memories alive for future generations.

Anne Loader
Léonie Press
March 2002

Contents

THE HORSEMAN'S TALE:
Farm and family life

ELIZABETH ELLEN OSBORNE

*I dedicate this story to my grandchildren Anthony and
Martin Gallimore, Paul Wood, Sarah and Lindsay Waller, and
to my great-grandson Mark Gallimore, who is now three years
old. I am afraid that this way of farming life will be to them
as the Iron Age is to us today. Everything is changing so fast,
and it will be nice to have the truth and first-hand information
about life on a farm in the late 19th and early 20th centuries.*

Nanna Osborne
EEO

Tea leaves, feather beds and clay pipes

My paternal granddad John Whalley was born about 1850 and lived in Winsford, He was one of quite a large extended family, but my sister Joyce and I didn't know all of them. I only remember Aunt "Mime" (Jemima), Dad's cousins Jane and Lily, and his cousins the Tomkinson boys, who only retired not long ago at a good age. They were great characters and ran a coal merchants' business in Winsford. They were well loved and liked for their kindness to their customers, always helping where they could.

Granddad married a Welsh girl, Jane Jones, and as far as I can gather they eventually moved to 50 Regent Street, Moulton, with one or two children. The rest of the family was born here, and as they grew up and started work they moved on to Crewe and other districts, got married and settled down. If I remember rightly there were four uncles (Bill, Joe, Ernie and George), four aunties (Lizzie, Mary, Annie and Harriet) and of course, my father, Charles Whalley.

My granddad worked long hours on the salt pans at Meadow Bank – a very hard and sweaty job. I remember seeing a photograph of him at work, stripped to the waist, with a red spotted kerchief around his neck and dark corduroy trousers tied with baling twine below the knee. He was fond of his pint of ale and his hobbies were keeping greyhounds, racing pigeons, and ferrets which he used to catch rabbits.

He often walked to see us at Shipbrook on a Sunday and would bring a couple of ferrets with him. He and Dad would go round the fields on a rabbit hunt and come home with more than one. After the family's needs were met the rest were sold at ninepence each. This was a price for so many goods when I was young.

Our Granny Whalley died of cancer when she was in her fifties. I can see her now: she was quite small against my grandfather's huge frame and she always wore black, which seemed to be the fashion in those days.

Of all those uncles and aunts in my Dad's family, my parents only stayed close friends with Uncle Ernie and Aunt Sally, and Aunt Annie and her husband Uncle Walter Daniels and their families. There were two children in the latter family, Walter and Annie Junior. Uncle Ernie and Auntie Sally had Alfred, Jack, Fred, Silas and Billy, Amy, Sally and Betty. Robert, the youngest, died when he was nine years old. Joyce and I still have a few cousins left from them.

Uncle Ernie joined up in the Army in 1914 and went through the war, finally being caught up in the terrible mustard gas attacks. I recall seeing him in his uniform when I was nearly four. He often told me how once when he came home on leave he visited Mum and Dad at Shipbrook and found me pumping water from Eyres' Pump onto my friend Patty, who was in the trough underneath the spout!

He was invalided out of the Army and was ill for a long time. When he was well enough to get a job he went to Brunner Mond's and again worked as hard as he could. My memory of him as he grew older was of a man who was always chesty and found it hard to breathe. He must have suffered terribly.

Aunt Sally was always someone special for us. They had known each other from the time Mrs Ann Latham had taken my mother, Elizabeth Scott, from a life of misery in the Workhouse to live with her at Moulton. I recall how my mother put great faith in her friendship.

When we went to Moulton we called on Aunt Sally and after our cup of tea Mum would say: "Would you read me the tea leaves?" Mother seemed to have great faith in the result. You had to swirl the almost empty cup round three times and then turn it upside down on the saucer to drain, then you waited to be told what the future held when the position of the leaves was interpreted for you. Readings might be: "You are going to get a letter in three days; you are going to meet a dark man; you are going to mix with some people at what looks like a party; you are going to receive some money – it will be a surprise". Even a few dark days were forecast, and we believed all this at the time. This faith was passed down to Joyce and me, and we often went in our teenage years to hear what the future held. Fortune-telling by cards, crystal ball or tea leaves was the fashion in our young days. Mrs Johnson from Leftwich was a great one for the crystal ball and a consultation cost 1s 3d.

Aunt Sally once told me that when she was a small child she lived at what is now Laburnum Cottage, Church Street, Davenham. It was just the old part when she was there – it has since been made into quite a big house.

She was a wonderful needlewoman: her crochet and lacework was beautiful.

After my dad left school I believe he went to work as a farm boy at Kinderton Hall Farm, Middlewich. He often told me how he 'lived in' and used to walk backwards and forwards to Moulton to visit his parents whenever possible.

I can't remember whether or not he stayed there until he went to Shipbrook Hill Farm to work for Mr Tom Parry, but if was from here that he got married to my mother. They went to live at Shipbrook Cottages. My mother called our house Rose Cottage and Mrs Robinson, at Number 4, called hers Ivy Cottage because it was covered in ivy. How I remember the many sparrows' nests that were in there. Mr Robinson used to take the old nests out when he trimmed the ivy and we would collect them and fix them in the hedge down the garden. We always thought that the sparrows would go to bed in them at night. What ideas you get as a child!

Dad would tell us how he and Mum got their first home together in 1912. Most of the furniture was bought from second-hand shops, Joey Allman's crooked-shaped shop at the bottom of Winnington Hill in particular. These items were all transported to their house at Shipbrook by horse-drawn cart or a lorry borrowed from the farmer. That is how they came by such lovely pieces as the rosewood and glass bookcase and cupboard combined, an oak corner cupboard, a sideboard, a

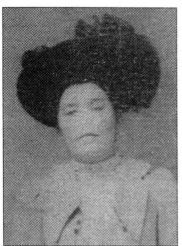

My mother Elizabeth in her youth. She bravely endured numerous painful operations on her nose and didn't like to have her photograph taken.

big polished table that stood in the centre of the front kitchen and six kitchen chairs. The ladderback armchair and rocking chair and a horsehair couch were all very comfy. There were also a couple of stools – all cottages had stools for small children to sit on in the evening. Over the fireplace was a beautiful mahogany overmantel – a mirror with fancy woodwork and little shelves at the front and down the sides. All these things would cost a fortune today! I believe some of them even came from the pawn shop, which was someone else's misfortune. Dad told me that their first bed cost a shilling and the mattress was made of horsehair.

I remember when I was quite young being wrapped up in a shawl and cradled in my mother's arms, being rocked back and forth in the old rocking chair. Another time I recall I had hot onions in a sock by my ear, fastened on with a piece of cloth round my chin and head. It was a great remedy for ear-ache when I was young.

I loved sitting on Dad's knee either being read a story or listening to one he was telling. These were very special moments because Dad didn't have a lot of spare time, working the long hours he did on the farm. The four of us often had a game of ludo or snakes and ladders, particuarly in the winter. Bear in mind that these sessions were short because it was 'early to bed and early to rise' with a lot of work to be done.

Mum and Dad used to earn extra money on occasions, especially at Christmas, by plucking turkeys, geese, ducks and fowl for the farmers, who paid them a pittance for this work. My mother never complained and it was this job that enabled her to make wonderful feather beds, pillows, bolsters and cushions. It was done by collecting all the feathers in pillowcases and stripping them by taking away the quills. The soft curled feather was then transferred to clean cases, tied up and put in a very hot oven. The fire would be stoked up to keep the oven at a high temperature for some hours. This was called 'stoving' and sterilised the feathers. Mother

My father - Charles Whalley - dressed up for my wedding in 1941

bought feather ticking – a blue-striped featherproof material – by the yard and width from Dodds shop in Crown Street, Northwich, and would sew each item up by hand.

We had all these at home. I remember that feather beds took over from flock mattresses, and they in turn replaced straw mattresses. I know people envied our lovely soft beds. We had such a lot to thank our mother for.

As I said in *"Nellie's Story"*, my dad was the mainstay of Shipbrook Hill Farm. He loved and lived for his animals. I recall him being sent for in the middle of the night in 1920 to go and collect sheep from the bottom Dane Meadow because the river had overflowed its banks after torrential rain. Even though he spent most of the night saving those sheep, he carried on with the daily work of milking to make sure the milk churns were on the early train at Billinge Green station. We didn't see him at all until late that night when all the stock was bedded down.

Another time he had a horse with very bad colic and he had to keep it walking round and round. I remember him saying:

"We darn't let it lie down." It ended being held up with a sling round its tummy to keep it upright. There were cows with milk fever too, and all the animals seemed to be treated with home remedies.

At a later date when he was working for Mr Cross, a mare was having a bad time giving birth to her foal. He stayed up all night with her and when he eventually came home he was so upset. He told us the poor mare had lost the battle and died. It took my dad a long time to get over that. This is very natural when you spend most of your time working in the fields with just your horse for company. Dad always said they were 'human' and understood every word you said. I recall once when he was telling me about the hard trails up and down the furrows behind the plough, harrowing or whatever, and he said: "You know, Dolly (his horse) gets tired too. We walk many miles together."

I often wondered how Dad walked at all when I saw the clay soil stuck to his shoes like crags. He had no money for the help of a chiropodist. Soaking his feet in salt water was the only remedy to ease them.

When I think back, I speak for hundreds of farm workers. They never worked fewer than 12 hours a day and often many more in the summer. My dad's wage at Parrys' was 25 shillings a week plus his cottage and one pint of milk each day. No overtime was paid and any extra milk was bought from Mrs Eyres for 1½d a pint. Joyce and I often had to go for it with a jug, and it was served from a pint measure with a handle on to hang it over the side of the big milk container. We also got eggs which Mother used boiled or scrambled, and for her cakes, bread and butter puddings, and egg custards.

On the subject of food, my mind wanders to Oxo and bread, and Quaker Oats and sugar in a bit of paper. We often took treats of cocoa and sugar from the pantry without our mother's permission!

Our pets during our childhood were a lovely dog called Jim and a beautiful snow-white cat called Snowball. He used to go and meet my mother from Parrys' Farm every time she came home. He seemed to know what time she finished work and would wait in the gateway to the field at the top of Shipbrook Hill. He always had a place at our table. He put his front paws on the side of the table and waited to be fed titbits. It was a very sad day for us when we found out that someone had shot him.

Jim lived to be 15 and then Dad bought us a spaniel puppy called Rover. He was a very mischievous puppy and I recall my mother saying "Rover will have to stop all this destruction or he will have to have a new home!" He had chewed the back out of one of my best shoes for one thing, and it cost 2s 6d to have a piece of leather sewn round the back so that I could wear them again. This was done by Mr Griffiths, our village cobbler. Rover did mend his ways and he also lived to be old.

This brings to mind stories of other folk's pets. I recall the harvest time when, I think, the Massey family from Little Leigh came along to each farm in turn with the steam-engined threshing machine to thresh the corn. Mrs Eyre's son Archie had a beautiful liver and white spaniel which followed him everywhere. When the threshing machine came to Mr Worth's farm Archie went along – like the other lads – with his dog to chase the rats which were disturbed when the crops were cut. Poor Archie never thought that his dog Jim would jump for one as it left the straw going into the bailer. Poor Jim was caught in the straw as it went down to be pressed into a bale and was crushed inside the machine. This was a great tragedy to both the men and boys and I understand after the day's work was finished they buried the bale, complete with Jim inside it. Even to all the neighbours it was like losing one of their family and Archie grieved for ages for his poor dog.

Dad had a double barrel gun and I know he used it to shoot rabbits and rats on the farm. He kept his gun at home and one spring day used it to kill a rat that had taken a tiny chicken from the pen. I watched in amazement as the rat ran across the garden and went up the sloping trunk of the apple tree. Dad fired and killed the rat but we couldn't save the little yellow chick.

Another time I watched a magpie and a crow fighting in flight over a little chick taken from Mr Eyre's hen-pen. It was a case of the crow having it and dropping it, and the magpie catching it and dropping it, and in the end it dropped into Eyres' Pit and was drowned. The pit was between Yew Tree Farm and the railway and was filled in by the council in later years.

These are sights you see once in a lifetime, if ever.

Although Dad liked a pint of beer, it was only very occasionally that he spent time at the 'local' on Saturday nights. He would walk to Davenham, spend an hour chatting to his mates over a couple of drinks and a game of dominoes, and then walk back to Shipbrook. It was early to bed and early to rise for him.

The Oddfellows and the Bull's Head pubs were both very dark smoky places in those days. I know because I knew Dorothy Platt at the Bull's Head and although I can't remember how I came to go in the Oddfellows, the smoke-filled snug room and the dismal green and brown painted walls still stick in my mind. I suppose the smoke came from the twist tobacco that was used in pipes – quite a lot of them made from clay. My granddad always had clay pipes and I've seen him chew tobacco, too. There were spittoons on the floor by the tables for the men to spit in. I think they held a certain amount of sawdust which helped to make them easier to clean.

Even though beer was quite cheap in those days, I know my dad didn't have much money to spend on it, as he also smoked a few Woodbine cigarettes. He gave them up some time before he passed away. That was his limit. I can honestly say that I never once heard bad language from either of my parents. They were just a simple God-fearing couple, getting on with the job of making an honest living and bringing up their family.

I remember my Irish Granddad Scott, a highly-skilled hedger

Shipbrook Hill – the seat was round the finger-post in the centre of the grass. Dad told me that a medieval castle used to stand on this site.

and ditcher, on one of his visits to our house during the evening, sitting by the fire with a tankard of beer at his side, taking up the poker, putting it in the fire, and when it was red hot holding it over the tankard and slowly dipping it in the beer until it sizzled. I understand it was a very popular drink. He would sit there, sipping and smoking his clay pipe filled with twist which he used to crumble up to fit in the tiny bowl. I hardly ever heard him hold a conversation: he just sat and browsed and after a few days' rest he would be off again on his wanders round the farms.

I know my mother seemed to be relieved to have a bit of peace because he often came in at teatimes really drunk, having spent time at the Bull's Head. I remember one day I was playing round the finger post seat at the top of Shipbrook Hill and I found quite a number of sixpenny pieces. I've often wondered if they were Granddad Scott's because I was told by the older girls that he frequently sat there on his way home from the pub and counted his money. To me it was a fortune and I gave the coins to my mother!

Yew Tree Farm, Shipbrook Road, Billinge Green showing hay being loaded on to the hay cart by Mr Harry Eyres and helpers.

A hard life for farm workers

The years went by, life went on in the same way and we still spent a lot of time at Parrys' Farm. One great interest was the kennels down the yard where a number of lovely greyhounds were kept. They had a special minder called Will, who lived in a room by the kennels. His job was to clean, exercise and feed the dogs. He had a bakehouse with a big oven and he baked brown bread daily for those dogs. Oh, it was a lovely warm smell down in that building! Old Will loved that job. I think the dogs were used for racing and it was a grand sight to see him out walking down Manor Lane with these differently-marked dogs, all on leads, several times a day, giving them their exercise.

I also wonder now what happened to Mr De'arden Jones who had a room at Parrys'. My dad respected him and he was always nice to my parents. I think I've got his name right but I don't know how to spell it. It was pronounced "DeHarden" or

"DeArden".

I don't recall my age at the time but I do know Belle Parry was older than me and we spent many happy hours at the farm. One day Mrs Parry asked my mother if she would allow me to go to the pictures at Middlewich as company for Belle to see a film. The hero was played by Rudolph Valentino and I think it was called "The Sheik". What I do know for sure is that poor Belle had what I understood was a crush on Valentino. I heard a conversation between Mrs Parry and my mother in which she said: "We're having a bit of trouble at the moment. Our Belle thinks he's wonderful!" My mum replied: "You'll have to watch her, at her age." At the time I didn't realise what they meant. I was allowed to go with her and was lent a bicycle. We rode along King Street and down the slope by the halfway house Belle had her feet up on the handlebars of her bike and was as happy as a songbird.

I sat through the film and didn't think much of it. I couldn't understand her being so wrapped up in what was nothing but a photograph to me! I now know that Valentino was the heartthrob of many teenagers. Poor Belle was on the point of running away from home over Rudolph.

I can actually count the times I went to the picture house, as we called it. I saw my first film, "Sonny Boy", at the Pavilion, and also "Tiptoe through the Tulips". I went to a Western and another film at the Plaza when that opened in Northwich, and I watched some sort of stage play at the Castle Picture House. That was it for me in my young days. I much preferred to be in the countryside.

Joyce and I missed the Brownies and the Guides because we lived too far away, and we never had time when we were in service to go to the village dance at the Assembly Rooms (now the dining room of the Bull's Head). I've only been to the Regal two or three times since that opened.

Thinking back to Parrys' farm I wonder if there are any of the Boy Scouts still alive who used to come with Scout Masters Jim Gregory and George Beaman to camp in the big orchard behind the farm? They had a very good time there. Jim Gregory later married Lizzie Parry – they were a lovely couple.

Time went on and Dad heard that the Parrys had money troubles. The rumour turned out to be true and they went bankrupt. There was a big sale and I was roaming round looking at the items on a table when I came across a lot of my own music sheets bearing my name, that had been lent to Belle when she was learning to play the piano. I told my mother and she said: "Never mind, love. There's nothing we can do now and they need the money."

My dad was told his services were no longer needed but Mr Parry said: "I have given you a very good reference for your work and loyal service to me and my family, and Mr Cross, who is taking the farm over, would be delighted if you would carry on in your present job and work for him."

This was wonderful news for Dad and a great weight off his mind, as he would have had to find a new job with a house for his family.

The Parrys left and went to Allostock to keep the Three Greyhounds public house.

I recall over tea one night my dad told Mum that Mr Cross had been discussing the wages he was to receive and had told him that Mr Parry had been underpaying him. By rights he could apply for back pay. Mum and Dad talked it over and Dad said: "Well, how can you ask for that? Look at the state they're in – they've no money." And so he told Mr Cross that he wasn't going to bother. That was Mum and Dad all over – always thinking of others' welfare.

I know Mr Cross gave him a rise but what it was, I'm not sure. Things went well for a number of years and Mother carried on cleaning the milk churns and cans and milking cows to help out. Eventually a baby girl arrived at the farm and was christened 'Julia'. When she got old enough she would come in the fields and play on the little hayricks. Joyce and I looked after her little haycocks which were shaken up and turned to enable the sun to dry the hay.

I remember a baby cousin of Julia's died at about two years of age. I know it was harvest time and I can see Julia now making a lovely hollow in one of the small haycocks and saying he was with Jesus, but that was a bed for him.

A few years later Mr Cross seemed to have things on his mind and became hasty and touchy. You never knew when he would fly off the handle. One bitter cold day Dad was ploughing a field and Mr Bill Wrench, Mrs Stubbs' farm man, was in the field on her land next to where Dad was. Mr Wrench called to Dad and asked "Have you got your tea can with you, Charlie?" Dad said "No!" "Right," said Bill, "when I come back down I'll give you a hot drink."

Dad thanked him and went on his way. On the return furrow Bill passed him a can lid of hot tea for which Dad was grateful. He had just got the can to his lips when a voice called out: "I don't pay you to drink bloody tea. Take a minute's notice, and be out in a week!"

I was there when my dad told Mother about it.

Dad was devastated and during the next night or so when he finished work he went out looking for a job with a house attached. He found one at Weaverham and the house was in Chapel Street, Castle, Northwich.

We moved in before the next week was out and it was bedtime before we had settled in because Dad had moved us after he had done his day's work. The first morning my mum got up and opened the back door to go and fill the kettle from the tap in a wash house which also held a toilet, across a tiny enclosed yard. It's true to say that my mum's heart was broken. She told me it was like being in a prison. No green fields, no birds singing – that was a sound Mum had lived with for years. The dawn chorus had been her music on the way to start her work at the farms.

Yes, her heart was breaking and Dad was out of his mind to see her fretting for the country. Then Fate took a hand. Mrs Frith and her daughter Edith who lived at Billinge Green Farm, Shipbrook, were looking for an experienced farm worker to

Ivy Cottage at Shipbrook has now been modernised

manage their land and stock. They got in touch with Dad and told him if he took the job Ivy Cottage at Shipbrook went with it. You can imagine my dad's joy to be able to take Mum back to her old haunts.

He explained things to his boss who pleaded with him to stay, but Dad couldn't do that and watch my mum die of a broken heart – because I certainly believe that is what would have happened.

We went back to Shipbrook and wasn't it Fate that we went to live in the house I'd spent so much time in as a child being looked after by Mrs Robinson and her family? It was my second home!

After all this upset my mother swore that she would do her best to try and save enough money to buy her own little cottage and not have to be turned out of house and home any more.

She got her wish a few years later when Mrs Frith and Edith retired. Mum bought a little cottage in Church Street, Davenham. I learned later that she borrowed £20 from Mr W

Carter at Gadbrook Farm for the deposit because it came on the market rather suddenly and it was just what she wanted. My dad got work at ICI through Mr Jack Spruce, who knew him, and he spoke for Dad, knowing he was a very conscientious worker. Mother paid that £20 back with interest because she worked many hours at Gadbrook for nothing besides the £20 she had saved up.

It was the happiest day of her life when she took up residence at 21 Church Street. There was a small garden, Harrop's orchard and the playing fields at the back, and she had her beloved birdsong once more. She said: "No-one will ever tell us to get out again!" and, God love her, she was happy there to her dying day.

As a footnote, I learned only recently that Bill Wrench was later treated in the same way by Mrs Stubbs over a very trivial thing. It was another case of: "Take a minute's notice and be out in a week." I must have been in service when that happened and it was his daughter, whom I hadn't seen for years, who told me about it. Farm workers certainly had plenty to put up with then, and life was hard.

During the hunting season there were nights when Dad would stay up and sleep in a chair until about 12.20am, then he would go out with a spade to block up the foxholes after the foxes had gone out on their nightly prowl. This meant that when the hounds started to hunt the foxes were unable to get back into their dens to hide. I know my dad was against this cruel deed but it was part of the work and, once again, it was a case of "do it, or else you're out of a job and house".

The weather made no difference. You had to carry on, rain, hail or shine and all the men working in the fields in bad weather had a very thick sack, or 'bag', as we called it, fastened round their shoulders and tied with baling twine. It was surprising how dry they kept – but just think of the weight it meant them carrying on their backs. A wet bag is a ton weight in itself.

In sickness and in health

Coming back to our Shipbrook days, after our lodgers left us, Joyce and I were able to share a bedroom. It was lovely, a big double bed with a soft feather bed you could almost lose yourself in, that had a good shake-up each day. It was like a big soft nest. Our bed warmer in the winter was either one of the big metal oven shelves or a building brick, wrapped up in a piece of blanket – sheer comfort! The pillows were the same sort of lovely soft down and by the side of the bed we had big pegged rugs to keep your feet off the cold oilcloth that covered the floor. I recall we got the oilcloth when I was about eight years old, before that it was scrubbed floorboards and pegged rugs, so you can see that it hasn't always been fancy carpets for the working classes: some poor souls didn't even have the warm rugs.

I have all my life, from an early age, loved to listen to what I call 'the sounds of nature'. Even silence has sounds if you listen carefully. Our bedroom window was partly open winter and summer, and I used to get out of bed and kneel by it. It's wonderful. I've heard cows crying for their calves after they were taken away from them, different birds like owls, peewits and curlews, and when I told my dad that I had heard a squeal down by Bluebell Wood he told me it was probably a wild boar. I can't verify this as I've read that they were supposed to be extinct some years before, but both Mr Parry and Dad said there had been a couple around for a short while.

When Mum came to bed and called in to make sure we were all right, she would say: "Come on, it's time you were asleep!" She called me a "night owl" and said I'd got to be up in the morning. I reckon I'm still a night owl. I'm still listening and looking, but there's only the cows' cry to be heard now in the distance; it's not the same living in a village that's all built up.

Owls are very rare around here now and it's years since I saw one. Skylarks, greenfinches, bullfinches – I haven't heard nor seen either. In my garden now our regular visitors are ring doves, wood pigeons, robins, blackbirds, house- and hedge-sparrows ('dunnocks'), and today I had a thrush, a rare sight. Magpies are plentiful and often rob the other birds' nests and take the young. This is our problem every year, but they are predators and Nature takes its course; there is nothing we can do about it.

I don't ever remember Joyce and me being allowed to go along the canal on our own, but when we were taken there was plenty to interest us. There was always water on the other side of the towpath because of the subsidence, and the ditches were great for finding sticklebacks, tadpoles and lots of other water creatures and plants. Dragonflies and fireflies also used to be very profuse. I've stood ages by the Briny fascinated by the movements of these beautiful creatures, but again, they are a rare sight today.

We would meet the narrowboats carrying salt and coal, being pulled by a horse, and there was always a greeting from whoever was steering the boat. Sometimes there were small children standing in the little opening leading to the cabin. These boats were the home of many families. It was a hard but wonderful lifestyle. I learned two beautiful poems when I was quite young, called 'Old Meg' and 'The Pedlar's Caravan'. When my cousin Nellie Clark used to stay over or I stayed at their house, we used to recite them and pretend we led the same life. Those poems were my solace during my first years in service.

Of the childish illnesses, Joyce had chickenpox and I got the measles. I had a habit of scratching the spots which used to itch terribly and Mrs Robinson (who looked after me during the day when Mum was working) bandaged my hands up to stop me. I can remember going down her garden and hiding behind the shed to have a good scratch. I got into trouble for that and had to sit on a chair so that she could keep her eye on me! I know now that it was for my own good. She also bathed my eyes in my own urine, which was supposed to be a wonderful cure...

While we had these illnesses, great care was taken that we were kept isolated from our friends so there were no visits from Aunt Milly, Nell and her sister Dora, but gradually things returned to normal. Uncle Joe, their dad, was a sick man after serving four years in the First World war and going back to his job at Littlers' Timber Yard in Northwich. He seemed to fail gradually and his heart weakened. He died at the age of 54, when Nell was 17 years old. Nell always loved my dad and I used to be jealous of her if I thought Dad took more notice of her than he did of me, but I realised later that her own father was too poorly to give his children the same attention. I'm glad now that I shared my dad's love with her.

As I mentioned, Nell has now passed away and that is another link of the chain gone. I feel sad at the passing of time. Of the immediate family there are only just my sister Joyce, myself and our cousin Dora left. I thank God for memories, for in the twilight of my life I can look back to all the happy times and live them over and over again.

I will tell you how illness was tackled in our Shipbrook days. Dad was taken ill when I was about nine years old and in those days it meant walking to Davenham to get hold of Dr Terry who had a surgery at the first bay-windowed house at the top of Church Street. It was also a small private nursing home. Nurse Hammond was in charge and she was held in great esteem by all and sundry. No one dared question her word! She was there for many years and was wonderful at her job. Anyway, Mother walked there to ask Dr Terry to come out to Dad and he told her that Dad was very poorly and would have to be nursed very carefully. So this meant that Mrs Robinson took over and helped my mother to nurse him.

I know they were talking very seriously one day and I heard Mrs Robinson say: "We will have to see if Charlie lasts the nine days' crisis. It's going to be a hard job – we must try to sweat the fever out of him."

Even though my dad had warm bricks and oven shelves he

was still very cold and shivering, so overcoats and even the huge pegged hearth rug was brought up to cover the bed. I know this because our bed was in the same room and Joyce and I had bedded down for the night.

Mrs Robinson's words to my mum were "If that doesn't do it, nothing will!" and she and Mum nursed him day and night. Although time meant little to Joyce and me in those days, when Mrs Robinson announced one morning "Thank God he's come through the crisis, he'll be all right now!" I did not understand what it was all about until we were older and it was explained to me.

I do remember how they got a big enamel bowl full of hot water and Dad was given a bed bath, clean clothes and clean sheets on the bed to make him nice and comfy. He was in bed for quite a while but got stronger every day. One of the 'pick-me-ups' they gave him was beef tea, which was used for invalids in those days.

We had another scare about a year later. My dad went to work one day as usual and we were told that night that he would not be coming home as he was in Manchester Royal Infirmary. It was thought that he had caught a dreaded thing called Anthrax from the cattle at the farm and he had to stay in quarantine until the tests had been checked. There was great relief amongst the family and neighbours when he came home with a clean bill of health.

We were all one close community and shared all good and bad times. One thing you could count on during sickness amongst the cottagers was cans of gruel and rich beef tea from the Rectory and Mrs Stubbs.

These incidents bring me to think of the stories my mother told me of the treatments used on her, like ether to put you to sleep and leeches to suck the blood, supposedly to take the poison away. How times have changed: it's strange to think that the humble aspirin has taken such an important place in modern medicine as it was the only thing we had to cure our pains in the old days.

Dad had teeth pulled out with pliers, and I remember well how I used TCP to heal my gums after my teeth were extracted when I was 22 years old, due to gum disease.

In those days some people had so little money that they were unable to save and plan for future events such as the birth of a baby. I recall one of our neighbours having her third or fourth child and she received the 'parish bag'. This was a charity bag – I'm not sure but I think it was a gift from the church. It contained the essentials to clothe a new baby.

It was also a rule that the new mother did not socialise until she had first paid a visit to church to be 'churched'. I don't know if it was a ritual in all districts but I do know it was kept up round here. I followed it myself when our children were born and my first outing was to church.

But back in our days at Shipbrook, Mrs Robinson was the stand-in midwife and she was very strict on these things. It was all part of life with us cottagers. Be it birth, sickness or death, she was there complete with huge starched snow-white apron and there had to be kettles and pans of boiling water ready at all times. We may not have had all the modern facilities but every care was taken to make sure that nothing was left to chance. The baby's bed was often a clothes basket or the bottom drawer of a large chest of drawers put by the bed to hold the new arrival, and babies spent a lot more time snuggled up close to their mother in her bed than they do now.

When any of our neighbours passed away, there was no chapel of rest, they would be laid out and a wooden door taken off its hinges and placed on a big table where the body would lie in state until the funeral – usually three or four days. During this time friends and neighbours, including children, would call in to pay their respects and look upon whoever it was for the last time. This went on mostly after the work for the day was done and a drink and refreshment was always on hand while people said their farewells to the deceased. We were all brought up to this and learned to cope with death at an early age. There was no fear of death.

Fancy hearses were rarely used when the farmers died – they were more often taken to the local churchyard by a horse-drawn lorry and it was surprising how people would walk behind this cortège. In certain circumstances you could hire the much cheaper bier which held the coffin and looked like a stretcher on wheels. It would be drawn and pushed by four or six bearers depending on the size of the coffin and the mourners would walk behind it. I have copies of bills for two funerals held years ago (see this page and the next) and they will give you a shock, I think, when you think of the price of such things today. However, one had a hard job to find even that small amount in those days.

Parish of Davenham.

Fees for the Burial of

Joseph Robinson

	£	s.	d.
Rector's Fee		6	0
Clerk's "		3	6
Sexton's "		2	6
For Taking up Gravestone		7	6
Grave Digging		15	0
Vault, or opening Vault			
Numbering Grave			
Extra charge for not being punctual to the time			
£	1	14	6

(Signed) *W E Cook*
Lower Parl Parish Clerk and Sexton.

Grave No. *504* Date *Nov.' 13ᵗʰ* 192*9*

N.B.—No Headstones, Tombstone, Monument, Tablet or other Gravestone will be admitted into the Churchyard until approved by the Rector, a design of any such, showing the dimensions, should therefore be submitted to the Rector before the work thereupon be commenced.

Glass Globes and Artificial Flowers cannot be admitted at all without a Faculty for the same being first obtained from the Consistory Court at Chester.

While on the subject of illness and death, and beliefs held by people, I must tell you of a couple of incidents that took place when I was 15 years old. Mr Robinson, our good friend and neighbour, was very ill and as usual it was a case of being nursed at home. This time it was my mother's turn to help Mrs Robinson to nurse her husband, doing nightly turns with Mrs Eyres.

At breakfast one morning, my mother was telling Dad it had been a troubled night and she didn't think Mr Robinson would be with us much longer as both she and Mrs Robinson had seen a robin fly right round the bedroom and settle on the bedrail. I asked how the bird had got in during the night, and my mother said: "Oh, it's an omen and you see these things before anyone passes away."

PARISH OF DAVENHAM.

------------ oOo ------------

FEES for the Burial of

Alice M Robinson

==

Rector's Fee		.	12
Clerk's Fee		.	7
Sexton's Fee		.	5
Churchwardens a/c	2		16
For taking up Gravestone & *Replacing*			15
Grave Digging			17 ⌐
Wheel Bier Hire			
Wheel Bier use of		.	1 ⌐
Vault, or Opening Vault			
Numbering Grave			
Extra charge for not being punctual to time			
		£	

£ 5 . 15 . 0

(Signed) *John Nickle*
Parish Clerk and Sexton.

Grave No. 504 .... Date *May 22 nd* 1944

N.B.,-No Headstone, Tomb-Stone, Monument,
Tablet or other Gravestone will be admitted into
the Churchyard until approved by the Rector; a design
of any such, showing the dimensions, should therefore
be submitted to the Rector before the work thereupon
be commenced.

Glass Globes and Artificial Flowers cannot be
admitted at all without a Faculty for the same being
first obtained from the Consistory Court at Chester.

Wheel Bier, Charge for Hire includes fee for use
within the Church boundary and Sexton's fee for
taking Bier to the house.

I thought about it and wondered.

Anyway, about a week later my mother and Joyce, my sister, were returning from a visit to Moulton. It was about 9.30pm and as they approached near to home they stopped in amazement as a ball of light appeared round from Eyres' house, floated around our house and up to Mrs Robinson's. It was about five feet from the ground and it did this circuit six times before they could move or speak, and then it disappeared. I understand my Mum's first words were: "I'll give Mr Robinson six days to live!" and he died exactly six days later. Even today, 72 years later, my sister swears this was true and that it still makes her blood run cold when she thinks about it. As for my mother, she definitely believed in things of this sort and took them in her stride.

This brings me to another story which both Mrs Robinson and my mother were to remember for a very long time. Both of them had been sitting up at night, as they called it, with a neighbour at the Canal House. They were both very tired and on edge. Mrs N passed away and the next step was to lay her out. Apparently the room was very small and the lady very large, and during the process of turning her over to get the old door in place to lie her on, she fell down between the bed and the wall and gave a big grunt. I understand they thought for a minute that she had called out but on reflection realised it had only been the wind leaving the body.

I know these happenings are very serious, but one can't help but see the funny side sometimes. I recall one neighbour on being told of the incident saying: "Yes, and I bet it put the wind up you pair!"

As for the omens, I don't treat them lightly because since I have grown older I have heard many people say they have had such experiences.

There were times when my dad repaired our shoes. He had a box which held a shoe last, bradawl, waxed thread, tacks, a very sharp pointed short-bladed knife, a stick of wax, thick needles shaped to get into awkward places, and a stick of black and brown stuff to make a good finished job.

I've kept a lot of these items in my shed and also among my treasures are different rug pegs which we used to make the rag rugs, crochet needles, knitting and a tatting shuttle. I never conquered using the shuttle, it was my mother's!

Amongst the linen I have pillow cases edged with crochet lace, huckaback towels and lace doilies which I use regularly.

My most treasured item is a waist petticoat made of fine cotton with a pocket quite low down in which my mother kept her little purse and handerkerchief. This slip is decorated with lovely broderie anglaise and must be over 100 years old. A very heavily embroidered long side serving table cloth is with it, which I often think would make a nice altar cloth for the church.

I have come across two old photographs, one taken at Yew Tree Farm, Shipbrook Road, Billinge Green (see page 10), showing hay being loaded on to the hay cart by Mr Eyres and helpers – one of whom could be my dad – and the other neighbours. Everyone helped with haymaking in those days.

Davenham smithy

The other one is very rare and shows the old smithy on the corner in the centre of Davenham village. It must have been taken between 1880 and 1900 but I can't identify anyone on it. I know the Pickering family ran the smithy in my young days. It is now the little garden on the corner by the Oddfellows pub.

Tucked away in the back of my shed is the scythe belonging to my dad that he used to cut the corn all round the edge of the field at the start of the harvest. He also cut nettles and other weeds with it. It can't have done his back any good and how his arms must have ached with the weight of it!

I recall one evening when Dad told Mother of the day's happenings at the farm, and he got quite het up about a new fertiliser which was to be used on the crops. His words ring in my ears: "It will be the ruination of farming. Food will never be the same again. There is nothing like the old muck-spreading with real farm manure!" How right he was.

Family feelings

My thoughts go back to childhood winter evenings with the glow of the oil lamp and the dancing flames of a coal fire, the kettle singing on the hob and the lovely voice of Irish tenor John McCormack coming forth from the big horned gramophone on the table. He was Dad's favourite singer and we all loved to hear him.

One of the favourite games we played was seeing who could find the most pictures made by the glowing coals in the fire!

Dad would tell us stories, especially in the winter when all the odd jobs were done straight after tea. These were tasks such as building up the fire, damping down coal dust to be put on top of the fire to make it last longer, and ensuring that there were plenty of buckets of fresh drinking water, coal and wood in for the evening and early morning. When all this was done we would settle down until bedtime – 9.30-10pm for our parents and earlier for us.

Dad told me quite a lot about the history of the castle which was supposed to have been built on Shipbrook Hill, how old Manor Farm at Whatcroft was, and also how Target Meadow by the River Dane got its name.

I often used to ask myself if these were all fairy stories but about a year ago I was lent some written records of the history of Davenham and district, and all Dad's stories are there in black and white.

Looking back, I see differences in the way words were pronounced. There were no short cuts and made-up sounds such as "gimme" instead of "give me". We had to speak English and pronounce it as such. Swearing was unheard of and there are words used nowadays that I never understood until I was well over 60 years old!

Our parents were so caring and our welfare came first. Even when I went out to work and up to when I was about 19 or 20 years old, my dad always saw me safely back to wherever I

My father in his old age

was living and then rode his bike home. He never grumbled about accompanying me and it was during these times together when I heard the stories about Vale Royal Abbey, Ida the Nun, Nixon's prophecies, and the Devil and St Chad's Church, Winsford. It was wonderful and the journeys passed so quickly.

My mind goes back to train trips to Northwich with my mother. When we arrived at the platform we had to walk up quite a lot of steps and we came out at the top of the station bridge. Across from the entrance were a few shops between there and Victoria Road. I recall a barber's, a cake shop, a bicycle shop, a shoe repairer and I think a paper shop, and on the other corner of Victoria Road was a cake shop where we used to have a cup of tea.

We would make our way down Witton Street and often call at Pop Hormbrey's to buy a drink of sasperella or ginger beer served out of big stone bottles. It was such a treat! As we carried on we would call at the Maypole to buy butter, where the assistant would cut a piece off a big block and shape it nicely with butter pats, leaving a pattern of a cow on the top. I think our last call was at the top of Crown Street to a little shop where we bought batch cakes. These were round bread cakes that you sliced down and were lovely with butter – a tea by themselves. They were in great demand and if you didn't get there early enough to buy some, they'd all be gone.

Although we were hard up, our parents would always try to treat us. I think Joyce and I would be about six and eight years old respectively when I recall us going down to town on the 'Dodger' train and walking down Witton Street at both Easter and Whitsuntide. We both looked with great awe and wonder at the lovely children's clothes in Mrs Birch's shop window –

26

yes, the same Birch's as today, but an older generation. It was full of pretty little dresses, bonnets and lovely straw hats all bedecked with little posies, lace and ribbons, little forget-me-nots and rosebuds. One week the colour would be yellow, another blue or pink and at Whitsun it was pure white.

I was too young to understand that Joyce and I were very lucky girls and I remember once being taken into the shop and being told we could choose a new dress and a straw hat. It was Easter and when my mother took us in I now realise that we were gently persuaded to pick the less expensive dresses. I found out later that my mother had to pay weekly for the goods. I will never forget a hat I took a fancy to. It was cream with blue ribbons tied at the back and little streamers hanging down. Entwined in the ribbons were forget-me-nots and a little yellow flower like a buttercup. The straw was so soft and silky! I used to rub my fingers round the brim.

I think we went to church a time or two during Easter and after that during the summer I played with Patty my friend, dressed up in my finery. The hat became a bit frayed at the edge and I discovered that it unravelled. I also found that when I took a piece between my teeth, to break it off, it tasted sweet. Believe it or not, after a time I had chewed up my straw hat, and all I had left were the ribbons and flowers! I asked Joyce the other day if she remembered me chewing my Easter hat up. "Yes, I do!" she said. "I also remember the trouble you caused." It was Patty's mother who got the blame for allowing me to be so destructive – apparently these clothes had been in her charge for some reason. I don't ever recall having another nice hat like that!

What memories – and I never dreamt that I would end up being a model for clothes for Mrs Birch and May Riley. I smile now: Nellie on the catwalk at Winnington Hall, the Memorial Hall, the chapel in Witton Street and the chapel on Castle. Happy days!

My dad never knew what holidays were and I remember

*My sister Joyce (right) and myself as we are today
– now 85 and 87 years old.*

when Sants came to collect the milk from the farm one of
the drivers took Dad for a run to Pendleton Dairies in
Manchester. They left about 8am on Sunday morning and got
back about noon, having delivered the milk and collected the
previous day's cans to bring back. I know Dad enjoyed this
odd trip.

Although life on the farm seemed hard, Dad used to say there
was much to compensate for this. He used to take us to collect
eggs from the stackyard sometimes when we were small and
the warm smell of the hay and straw was lovely.

Those were the days of fresh-laid eggs, dark and brown, and
don't forget the beautiful colours of the duck eggs. We had four
'upside-down' egg-cups – one way up for hen's eggs and the
other for duck's eggs. They are here in my cupboard now, in
perfect condition, and are marked "Grindley, England". I
would love to know how old they are.

Winters came and dark nights were long, we had no electric

lights on all night like you do today. In December I can hear my mum saying: "Come two weeks after Christmas you'll see it getting lighter, a cock-stride a night!" How true those words are. I don't suppose the youngsters of today would understand what that expression meant, not having seen a farmyard full of hens and a huge red cockerel strutting round.

Not long ago, I found myself watching a programme on ITV called "The Last Horseman" which was so evocative that I thought I must be dreaming. I was "with" my dad, seeing him with Dolly his horse busy ploughing, harrowing, spreading muck and sowing the seed – all done with the same implements. I saw the same scenes, the farmyard with a cat strolling round and the old house pet dog curled up in an armchair.

I could see Dad breaking a horse, stroking and loving it. You could see the horse's ear shake to show he understood. It was a marvellous half-hour and I spent it in my mind all around Parrys' Farm and the fields of Shipbrook. I've slowly come back to find that I'm sitting here in the twilight of my life with my husband Ralph. I'm not ashamed to say that my tears are falling as I write this, not because I am sad but because I'm happy and thankful that God has given me the wonderful gift of my photographic memory.

THE APPRENTICE MECHANIC'S TALE:
Brought up on the Tip Bonk

GEOFFREY MELLOR

I would like to dedicate this to:
my Mum and Dad, and my sister Jean;
Mr H S Smith, who taught me to read and play music;
and to Mr Harry Breeze who put me right
about the motor trade.
GM

A sturdy little lad

My story starts before the Second World War. My mother told me that I was one of twin boys, born on 17th June 1934 in St Mary's Hospital, Manchester. Unfortunately, my brother died after six hours. I was ten days old when we came home to my grandparents' house in 16 Egerton Terrace, Altrincham, Cheshire. When I was one year and eleven months old, my sister Jean Grace was born, on 21st May 1936. The 'one year and eleven months' seemed very important to my mother because in those days if you didn't wait a decent time between having children, you were branded a sexpot!

I don't remember much about my life with my grandparents, but my mother said I was a sturdy little lad who fought my own battles. One story she told me was about two bigger boys playing in a puddle with me and wetting me through, so I got a branch of a tree and soaked them by splashing it in the puddle.

My father worked as a builder's labourer and had to mix the mortar, using lime which was kept in a lime pit. When we took his dinner round to him they wouldn't let me play in the yard in case I fell into the pit.

We left Altrincham when my father got a job and a house – 8 Hewitt Street – at Lostock Gralam near Northwich, Cheshire. At the age of four years, I started my life at 'Bottom Lostock'.

The first streets from the Northwich direction were Austin Street, Hewitt Street and Renshaw Street, which were known as the 'Tip Bonk', and Boundary Street, Victoria Street and Brook Street, which were known as the 'Smut Bonk'. If you looked from the canal bridge down towards Northwich, on the left was Hesketh Mill, then the black and white Victorian infants' school, and then Stanley Grove. Lower down came the Methodist Chapel, some terraced houses, and then the entrance to Lostock ICI which was called Works Lane. Down Works Lane were the entrance to Lostock ICI Social Club, the Cenotaph and the Scout Hall.

In Hewitt Street, starting from the top left, was Jimmy Mailham's bike shop, the Northwich and Winnington Co-op, four houses which were occupied by the Billingtons (No. 1), the Illages

(No. 3), the Inglefields (No. 5) and the Greens (No. 7), then an open space where the houses had been knocked down, which was our play area. On the right was Wakefields, which was on the main road but the yard ran down Hewitt Street. In our block, which consisted of six houses, the families were the Dickens (No. 2), the Lambs (No. 4), the Whiteheads (No. 6), the Mellors – us (No. 8), the Lambs Jnr (No. 10) and the Joneses (No. 12). Next was the Bonk which had been a tip years ago, before the houses where we lived were built. We used to play there, too. Over the Bonk, allotments led down to the Wincham Brook. I was told that its real name was the River Eye. The allotment holders along the brook kept hens, ducks and geese that they fattened up for Christmas and sold to the neighbours.

I remember that Jimmy Mailham, who mended bikes, always worked in a collar and tie. He started work at 9am and finished at 5pm.

When we moved in, I had to get to know the children around us, who were a bit wary because we were new. Most of the other families were related in some way. We always addressed the adults as 'Mr' and 'Mrs', which we were told to do. When I came out of the house one day, I was hit in the left eye by a stone and had to be taken to the eye hospital at Manchester. I remember coming back over the canal bridge and the driver letting me ring the bell. After that everyone seemed to be very friendly and the boys of my age started to call for me to go out and play.

It was soon time for me to start my education, so my Mam took me to the infants' school in Manchester Road. I remember on the first day a girl hit me because she didn't like the way I looked, so I hit her back. The teacher, Miss Hall, struck me across the hand with a ruler and said: "Boys don't hit girls".

The head teacher was 'Big Miss Blower', her sister 'Little Miss Blower' was her deputy and Miss Paulden was the scripture teacher. I think Miss Paulden liked me because I seemed to find her lessons fairly easy and I came top of the scripture class with Anne Storey every time.

We had not started school long when the war started. In wartime we couldn't get Christmas decorations so we had to make our own. Mam would get some crepe paper and we would cut it up into strips about six inches long and glue it with paste which we made with flour and water. We would get holly from Wincham Hall and put it around the pictures. We also made a 'kissing bush' by crossing two hoops, wrapping them with different coloured crepe paper and hanging silver paper and little trinkets from them. When it was done we would string it up in the centre of the living room. Mam would pay so much a week so we could have a good Christmas – and we always did!

On Christmas Day she would cook us a breakfast of egg, bacon, sausage and fried bread. Dinner was chicken with potatoes, sprouts, turnip, cabbage and gravy, followed by pudding and custard. For tea we

Me as a young boy

had butties, mince pies and jelly with more custard.

On New Year's Eve, Dad would go out of the back door at 11.55pm with the Old Year. At 12.05am on 1st January Dad would knock at the front door and Mam would let him in with a kiss. He would give her a shilling, a piece of coal and a loaf of bread so we could have a prosperous New Year.

We took the decorations down before the 6th January because it was supposed to be unlucky to leave them up after that day. However, we used to leave the holly around the pictures till Pancake Tuesday and then burn it under the pan on the fire.

At the beginning of the war we were each given a square brown box that contained a gas mask which we had to learn to use. The council had built two air raid shelters and there was a Air Raid Warden who kept them locked and opened them when the sirens sounded. We knew the siren as 'Moaning Minnie'. Our neighbour Mrs Whitehead had a young baby and had a big gas mask that she put the baby in. She had to use a pump for the air. We all went to have a look.

We had to take our gas masks to school and we did air raid practice. We had to go into the air raid shelters when the siren sounded, then when the teachers shouted "gas attack" we had to put the gas masks on.

We stopped getting toffee from the shops and the fruit we had was grown locally. We all "dug for victory!".

On a Saturday we went to Nobby Griffiths' farm to pick potatoes and to help with other farm jobs like mucking out, and cleaning the sheds and stables.

We used to go down Works Lane and through Bucks field to the canal, over the bridge and across the fields to the farm. One of the cows must have thought she was a bull because she often chased us and we would escape up the lime beds.

My sister and I didn't see much of our dad because he was working at ICI, served in the Home Guard and was also a reserve fireman. I felt a bit sorry for him, because when he was 14 years old and left school he started work as an apprentice mechanic. But he caught rheumatic fever and had to stop work. He was about 19 years old before he was allowed back to work again, but by then it was too late to carry on with the apprenticeship. Anyway, he joined the Territorial Army, became a lance-corporal and when the war started he wanted to join the Army. He tried to get in at Chester, Warrington, Manchester, Crewe and Stoke-on-Trent but was refused entry because of the fever he'd had when he was younger.

Our home at 8 Hewitt Street was a three-bedroomed house. You went through the front door into the living room which was lit by gas. On the left was a four-paned sash window and round to the right was the big cupboard where we kept food, crockery, pots, dusters, Brasso and shoe-cleaning things. We used to put old newspapers in the bottom of the cupboard where all the cockroaches made their nests. On 5th November I would get the papers out of the cupboard and burn them on the bonfire with the cockroaches and nests inside. When the papers were alight you could hear the cockroaches crackling as they burned. It was cruel but it was the only way to get rid of them.

Beside the cupboard was the oven, with two steel oven plates which served as shelves and were used to warm our beds in winter. Also in the oven were two house bricks which heated our parents' bed. Next to the oven was the fire grate and the hob, where a kettle filled with water was kept so that we had hot water all the time. In the back kitchen was another fire grate which we didn't use very often. Mam used the boiler in the corner to boil the clothes on Monday mornings – wash day. The sink was a brown trough with a cold water tap over it. She had a mangle for wringing the clothes out after they had been washed in the dolly-tub with a dolly-handle. This was like a four-legged stool with a handle that was put in the water with the clothes and turned in a rotary motion to get the washing clean. In the corner of the sink was a tea strainer so we could empty the tea leaves out of the tea pot into it without blocking the drains. We put them on the garden.

Along to the right was the back door which led to the back yard. There was another door to the stairs and then a door to the coal house under the stairs, where we went to shelter later on in the war.

When you went through the back door into the yard, the lavatory was at the bottom on the right, with a tin under a wooden seat. It was emptied on a Tuesday night, with all the others in the area, by the council night shift who got extra pay because it was a dirty and smelly job. The men came round with a horse and cart which was like a tank on wheels.

Most of us kids played games all together. One of our games was 'Kick the can', where a tin can was placed in middle of a square and then someone was picked to be 'on'. The other kids had to hide, and you then had to find them. When you caught them they had to stay in the den until someone 'snook up', kicked the can and released everybody. 'Deleavo' was a similar game but instead of kicking the can you had to touch the wall and shout 'Deleavo!'. Most of the games seemed to be seasonal or whatever took our fancy from the pictures like bows and arrows, and cowboys and Indians. Other games were 'top and whip', hopscotch, skipping, roller-skating and catapulting.

The war didn't seem to worry us kids too much – perhaps we

were too young to understand what it was all about. When the siren went, we hurried into the air raid shelters then had a good singsong and a brew until it was all over and the 'all clear' sounded.

When summer came we used to go to the River Eye to swim below the waterfall. We called it Wade Brook where we learned to swim. The big lads wouldn't allow us to swim in the river but they let us go in Polly Park's which was about 3ft deep. When you thought that you could swim, a couple of the big lads would test you and if they said OK then you could swim in Wilson's and the Gardens, which seemed quite deep. When we broke up from school for the summer holidays we would put on our swimming trunks (which were home-made out of an old pullover or jersey) and that was all we usually wore while we were swimming and messing about in the woods. We never used a towel – when we had been swimming in the river we would run about to get dry. We became very brown and felt great.

When we became hungry we would dig in the river bank and about four inches down we would find roots which we would peel and wash off in the river and eat. They tasted rather like chestnuts but a bit sweeter. We knew them as 'pignuts'. Also we would swim across to the gardens to get apples, pears and potatoes which we would cover in clay from the river bank and bake in a fire that we had lit earlier in the day.

Down from Wilson's was a little stream that ran into a pond which we called the 'duck islands'. When you paddled in the water, it was about 3ft deep and always felt warm. If you reached down into the black mud you could find freshwater oysters. We would split them open and look for pearls, like we'd seen people do in the films, but we never found any!

When winter came and we'd had about three days' hard frost, the ponds and pits were usually safe to slide on, and out came our steel-tipped clogs, so we could 'skate'.

Our parents used to buy us boots to wear for school and for playing out, and when they were worn out we had them soled, heeled and studded. After they had been mended about three times, the uppers were made into clogs by the cobbler, whom we knew as Clogger Booth.

We had to make things last because they were rationed and hard to obtain. We had coupons for food, clothing, meat and sweets – when you could get them. Our family didn't have petrol coupons because we didn't have a car, and anyway most cars were laid up because of the war.

My best friend was Neil Anderson, who lived across the backs, and we played together most of the time. We played football in the little field across Manchester Road. The big lads wouldn't let us play on the big field till we were about 12 years old. The field was owned by ICI and a farmer called Arthur Platt rented it. He kept cows that were in calf and Shire horses in the same field. When one of the cows had a calf, we had to ring Pickmere 21 and he would come and collect the cow and calf and pay us 2s 6d (12.5p). In this field the pipes that carried brine and lime waste between Lostock and Winnington Works ran through a tunnel under the road. It was a nice place to be on a winter's night because it was warm from the heat of the pipes. In the field were three ponds known as 'Big Ben' (near the railway), 'the Oily', near Mid Cheshire Oil Company and 'the Froggy' where we got frogspawn, newts and little fish we called 'Jack Sharps'. Their real name was 'sticklebacks'. Once, one of the Shire horses fell in 'the Oily', so we rang Mr Platt and he got the Fire Brigade to rescue it. He gave us five shillings (25p) because the horse was more valuable than a cow and calf. In this field we also found mushrooms which were nice to eat when they were fried.

A rag-and-bone-man came round every week collecting old clothes, pots and pans, and anything else that he could sell. In exchange for what we gave him he would give us donkey stones and little toys he had made. Our mothers used the donkey stones to clean the front doorsteps and keep the edges of the steps white. We got to know him quite well because he was a nice man. The adults knew him as Billy Carley, but we had to call him 'Mr Carley'. He had a yard at the back of Victoria Street where he stored the stuff he had collected. We sometimes went on his rounds with him and helped him with his pony and cart. In the mornings when we went to the yard we would feed the pony – a Welsh Cob – and then when he had finished eating we would harness him to the cart, ready to work. At night when we came back to the yard we took him out of the cart, unharnessed him, put him in the stable and groomed him. When he had cooled down, we had to feed and water him, and bed him down for the night. We knew that if he had water while he was still hot it would make him ill. We would then clean the harness with a cloth and hang it up ready for the next day.

We had a little black and white mongrel bitch called Judy. In the next street lived her sister who looked very similar and was left to roam about freely most of the time. We kept our Judy in the house and back yard and were very surprised when Sgt. Blithe came to see us one day and said that our dog had killed 20 hens in one of the allotments. Sgt. Blithe said that my dad would be prosecuted. Dad was very worried about this. Anyway Mam said if that was the case the hens were ours. So he brought them round to our house and Mam, Jean and I plucked them and Mam gutted and dressed them and then sold them to the local butcher for a pound each – which was a lot of money in wartime. The people who bought them didn't suffer any ill effects. When Dad went to court he was made to pay £1 fine, so Mam made £19 profit and we also knew it wasn't our Judy anyway. I always thought that our Mam was very clever and if she had received a normal education she would have done very well.

We had a wireless which didn't have a case on it and I soon understood why – it was so that the valves could be removed and it wouldn't work when the detector van came round.

About this time our Judy had pups and I took one of my mates home to see them. She must have thought he had come to take them so she chased him and bit him on his bum. I had to go to the post office for a dog licence in case his parents reported us to the Police – but she was only protecting her pups.

When I was about six years old Neil and I joined the Tip Gang and to get in you had to swarm along the pipe tunnel which was about 16ft long. We all played well together. We made catapults and we would go down to the pipe bridge at Wade Brook, pick two sides and then go either side of the bridge and fire duck stones at each other. It's a wonder one of us didn't lose a eye or something worse. One day I was playing by myself on the pipe track and I found a safety valve. I discovered that if you hit the ball with a brick on one side a jet of brine would shoot up in the air. Neil had been to see his auntie and had come to find me. I told him what I had found and showed him what to do, but I warned him not to do it because he had his best suit on. As usual he wouldn't be told and had to see if it worked – which it did and covered his new suit in brine. Of course he blamed me and ran home crying to tell his dad what I had done to his suit. They came back looking for me and I was frightened because I thought his dad would hit me for spoiling Neil's suit. Most neighbours were allowed to hit you if they caught you doing wrong or being cheeky and they usually gave you a clout around the earhole. It wasn't any good telling your own dad because he always believed the adults, anyway, so you would get another clout off him. I said a little prayer and asked for help, and a voice entered my head telling me to go through the pipe tunnel and follow the pipe track up to Works Lane, then across Manchester Road and down the backs to our house where I knew I would be safe. Our mother wouldn't let anybody hit us know matter how big they were.

I remember one day Neil and I had been fighting, as young lads do, and he ran home crying to his mother. She came over to our house carrying a cricket stump and shouting about what she was going to do to me. In the end she broke the front window with it. My Mam went out and a fight started. Mam, being bigger, took the stump off her and hit her with it to see how she liked it. While the two mothers were fighting Neil I were playing football togeth-er down the backs. After that our parents decided not to fall out over us kids again but to let us get on with it and sort things out for ourselves.

What upset Mam most was that we couldn't get any glass dur-ing the war so we had to cover the window up with cardboard which let in a draught and the rain – and also allowed some light out.

When we had to fight anybody, we would usually talk about it first unless it was a heat-of-the-moment fight. If it was discussed first it was usually agreed to stop at 'first blood' which was nor-mally a cut lip or a bleeding nose, or when one said they'd had enough. Then the fight would stop and we would shake hands and carry on playing together as though nothing had happened –

not like today when they want to kill each other!

Our Mam's name was Jane and she was brought up by her grandmother until she died and then they put her in an orphanage. One day we all went to the pictures to watch "Jane Eyre". One scene showed a girl being punished for something she had done wrong. She had to walk round the school playground in the pouring rain with a notice around her neck saying what she had done, and Mam said that was what it had been like in her day – very cruel. When she left the orphanage she went to work on a farm. She had to feed the hens, look after the pigs and bring the cows up to be milked by hand, not by machine as is done at present. She told us that the pigs would know when they were going to market to be sold or slaughtered because they would start squealing and no matter how much you fed them they wouldn't eat. When she left the farm she went to work at Hefferston Grange in Weaverham as assistant cook. I remember her telling us about the 'Lady in White' who was supposed to haunt Hefferston Grange with her black Labrador. She appeared at the bottom of Mam's bed one night – she was very frightened and hid under the bed covers. It could have been a story but we believed her. She then went to work at Altrincham General Hospital as assistant cook. That's where she meet Aunty Grace who introduced her to our dad. They courted for six months and then they got married.

Our Mam was very proud of coming from Warrington. 'The Wires' was the nickname for Warrington because of the local wire works. She was a very tough lady as a result of being brought up in the orphanage and she wouldn't let anybody bully us. I remember one day when our Jean and I were playing 'tick' and as we ran up the backs some kids were playing skipping across the backs. As I ran up they dropped the rope so I could pass but when our Jean came to pass I heard a woman tell them to pull the rope tight and trip her up. They did and she fell over, cutting her knees very badly. I had to take her home and tell Mam what had happened. Mam went across to ask about the incident and when she got there they were all laughing about tripping Jean up. But the woman soon stopped laughing when Mam hit her: she went the full length of her yard and fell over. She said she would tell her husband when he came home from work, so Mam said to bring him and his mates and she would sort them all out. When her husband came over Mam went out to meet him and we were worried because he was a big man. But there was no need to worry because he shook hands with Mam and said he had wanted to do that to his wife for years.

Afterwards it was time for our weekly bath, so out came the tin bath and it was put in front of the fire and filled with hot water out of the kettle and pans. Jean went first because Mam said that I was the dirtiest so I had to go second. After the bath it was time for Syrup of Figs to keep us regular and then it was 'nit time'. Newspaper was put on the table and the nit comb was used to comb our hair. Jean went first and if any came out on to the paper I would crush them with my thumbnail and our Jean would do mine. She usually had more than me because her hair was longer than mine.

One day when Neil and I were out playing, his mother called him in for a cup of tea and a piece of jam tart, and asked me if I wanted to have some too. We went into their house and she gave us the tea and tart – but she didn't say it was a marmalade tart. I had a bite of it and when I tasted it I didn't like it, so I broke the crust off, stuck the rest under the table and then I ate the crust. When Mrs Anderson came back into the living room and saw that I had finished the tart she offered me another piece, which I swiftly refused, and Neil and I went back out to play. About three days later Mrs Anderson stopped Mam in the street and told her what I had done. Mam said she should have told me it was marmalade tart instead of jam tart because I didn't like marmalade. They both had a good laugh about what I had done.

When I was seven years old I had to leave the infants and go to St John's Church of England School in School Road, Lostock. We were taught about scripture and learnt to pray, sing hymns and how to act in church. There was no wearing of hats or caps, and no whistling or swearing; we always had to go neat and tidy. We learnt the Lord's Prayer and "All Things Bright And Beautiful", which was and still is my favourite hymn. I met a lot of new children at the school. I was bullied a bit because I was rather small for my age. When we were playing football and picked sides so that we had two teams to play against each other, I was usually picked last because I wasn't very good. Sometimes I was left out altogether and had to be the ball boy.

When I was going home from school one night I found a fountain pen which I took home and my dad said I should take it back to school next day in case it belonged to someone there who had dropped it. I forgot – however, somebody had seen me pick it up. The teacher accused me of stealing it and said he would have to punish me, to teach me it was wrong to steal. But my dad had found it on the table at home and realized that I had forgotten it, so he decided to bring it to school and arrived just in time to save me from the cane. The teacher never apologised for accusing me of stealing the pen but when he went red and looked very guilty I was quite happy.

One day I had a fight with lad called Hubert. I gave him a good hiding and he said he would tell his big brother who would do the same to me. Well, the next night Hubert and his brother Luggy were waiting for me. I was very scared because he had a reputation for being a good fighter and was also about five years older. When he told Hubert to hit me I plucked up courage, hit Luggy in the stomach and ran home as fast as I could. The next night when I came out of school they were waiting for me and so I thought "Here we go again" but it wasn't so. This time Luggy said he wasn't going to hit me because I was a brave little kid. After that Hubert and I became good friends and started to play together at playtime and dinner time because we both stayed for school dinners. When what had happened got around school, the people that had bullied me soon stopped. It's surprising what happens when people think that you can fight, and I seemed to have more friends than I had before.

Every so often we went to Lostock Works canteen for dinner instead of going home and we had our dinner with the workmen around the back of the canteen in the big dining room where there was a stage at one end. The workmen were entertained by some of the well-known entertainers of that time including Arthur Askey, Tommy Handley, Ted Ray and George Formby.

After the war had been on for about three years, I think most people had started to relax. We stopped going under the stairs

My sister Jean, my father, my mother and myself

and stayed in the front room when the siren sounded. We had a singsong while Dad was doing his duty patrolling the streets. Although Mam couldn't read or write she had a very good memory and taught us a lot of old songs which we sang till the 'all clear' sounded.

There was an anti-aircraft gun at the bottom of the wood and when we went to talk to the soldiers who manned it they gave us some fruit, jelly and cream. They told us that they had to defend I.C.I. and the British Octel Company at Plumley. Our dad got a job at 'The Octel', as we called it, making anti-knock compound for aircraft fuel which was very important to the war effort. Because he was working with a lot of lead he had to have his urine and stools checked every month for lead content and a company car would deliver a brown paper bag to our house containing a large glass jar and also a small bottle to hold the 'by-products' of Dad's food and drink.

About this time I joined the Cubs at 3rd Northwich Wolf Cub Pack – mostly so I could have a proper bath at the Scout Hall on a Wednesday night after the Cub meeting!

My mate Neil went to live in Rudheath and started at Victoria

Road School and so I had to find a new friend. He was Tom Jones, not the famous singer but the one who lived near us at Number 12. We got on very well together and went farming at Arthur Fryer's farm in Green Lane, Wincham.

It was time now for us take the 11-Plus Exam to see if we were clever enough to go to Sir John Deane's or Winsford Grammar School. I knew my parents couldn't afford to send me to either of them so on the day of the exam I wrote my name and the date on the paper and then sat there until it was time to go home. Obviously, I didn't pass and I had to go to Rudheath Modern Secondary School for Boys. To get to school we went down Works Lane past the Scout Hall and through Bucks field along the canal then down Farm Road. I remember the first day quite well because somebody said that the lads from Wincham School were better fighters than the lads from Lostock School. Some bright spark suggested me to fight one of their lads to see who was best. I didn't want to fight but I couldn't back down and be called 'yellow' so we had a fight and made a draw. This satisfied everybody and I made another mate. After that we all got along fairly well together and used to play football at playtime in the school yard until someone broke a window and all ball games were banned.

When we went along the canal to school you would sometimes pass the heavy horses pulling the canal boats or 'cut boats' as we called them. (The 'cut' was the nickname for the canal.) The last bridge before Farm Road was called Milky Bridge, where the towpath was very narrow, and if you were unlucky enough to meet a big horse under the bridge there was only one way to go – and that was into the canal! When you got knocked into the canal you had to get to the side so the boat could pass. If you were on a bike you would have to get your bike out of the canal afterwards and then when you arrived at school wet through you would get the cane for being late.

I hadn't been at Rudheath School long when Mr. W. H. Smith, the head teacher, announced that anybody who would like to learn to play the recorder should report to his office. Because I couldn't sing very well I decided to go along. When I got there I found six more lads who also wanted to learn to play the recorder. The headmaster was very pleased to get so many who were interested. He started off by giving us a recorder each to play and he taught us the scale of C first, which was quite difficult. You had to cover all the finger holes on the recorder then remove them one at time to get the different notes and who ever could play up and down the scale the fastest by the following week would get a half a crown (2s 6d) – which was a lot of money, or so it seemed at the time. So I practised very hard every chance I got, which annoyéd the neighbours a bit, but I won the money. My first recorder cost 7s 6d (35p) for which I paid 2s 6d down and then a shilling a week and sixpence for the last week. While I was learning to play and read music so that I could join the school pipe band, I would go down to the woods to practise. I was a bit shy when people came past and stopped playing. But I climbed a tree and hid then I started playing again when the people had gone past. I think they thought it was the Little People!

When Mr. Smith decided that you were good enough to play in the school pipe band you could go to Band practice when the class had a music lesson. We learned the hymns which we played every morning in the School Hall for assembly.

One day at school we were playing 'tick' in and around the toilets – which was forbidden. As I ran into the toilets, I ran into Mr Dunn and knocked him over. He told me to go to his classroom for the cane and wait for him. When I got there, there was already a line of lads also been caught playing 'tick' in the same place. Mr Dunn was a very fair-minded teacher and he said if you had a good reason for being around the toilets you would be let off. So when it was my turn to explain, I'd had plenty of time to think of a good excuse. I told him that I had been taken short and had to go fast – because after I had knocked him over I'd run into a cubicle, locked the door, sat on the toilet seat for a bit and then pulled the chain. He had stood outside the toilet door listening, so he believed me and let me off.

Scouts, school and Smiler

By this time I had been in the Scouts about two years, during which time I had earned some badges for First Aid, cooking, woodcraft and also my second Class Scout Badge. We were soon going on our first Camp to Trout Hall Farm at Plumley for a long weekend to get us ready for our week's Camp in North Wales. Plumley was about three miles from where we lived in Bottom Lostock and we were going to take our luggage on the trek cart. But first we had to know how to take it to pieces which we soon learned and eventually we could strip it down and put it back together in about two minutes flat. On the day we were going to Plumley we loaded up the trek cart with our belongings, cooking utensils and the tents and away we went, with two Scouts pulling on the T-shafts and four Scouts pulling the ropes that were fastened to the axle on either side. We had to take it in turns, pulling till we got to where we were going to camp for the weekend.

When we arrived at the campsite we had to put up the bell tents and dig a large deep hole for the latrine. The bell tents were quite easy to erect. You got the tent out of the bag and laid it on the ground, then two Scouts put the centre pole into the canvas tent and four Scouts got the four main guide ropes and on the word of command the two on the pole lifted the pole up and the four on the guide ropes pulled the tent up and pegged the ropes down. When that was done we put the rest of the pegs in, then we put the groundsheet in the tent and picked where we were going to sleep. Being one of the smallest I usually had to sleep by the door. But what the others didn't realise was that I wasn't getting any bad smells from their sweaty feet and farts! We all enjoyed camping but it was a bit cold in the mornings having to wash in the brook. It was a good job we didn't have to shave.

Scout night was on a Wednesday night at seven o'clock. We all stood in a semi-circle to see who was present and who was missing and then we said the Scout Promise that I still know to this day. While we were saying the Scout Laws the Union Jack was unfurled. After the roll call we would go to our corners to study for more badges and for the First Class Scout badge – which I didn't get. When we had been dismissed at about nine o'clock we would go to the Outdoor House that was owned by Miss Riley, whom we called 'Mother Riley' behind her back. We would buy some pop (Tizer, lemonade or dandelion and burdock) and then we would go under the canal bridge to drink it.

When I was 11 years old the war in Europe ended and was celebrated in many different ways. The first I knew about it was when Dad woke us up and told us it was over and to get dressed. We all went to Manchester Road and when we got there it was full of people singing and dancing – this was about five o'clock in the morning. The adults organised street parties and the streets all had tables and chairs with table cloths on them. We had to sit down around the tables and then the food was brought out. I don't know where it all came from but I hadn't seen as much in all my life. We all tucked in and had our fill. After the party we had games like 'pass the parcel' and other games that the adults knew which we soon learned how to play.

After VE-Day things settled down to normal – whatever that was. The war in the Far East was still being fought but because it was so far away we didn't really bother about it. When I went back to school I was in 1B but when we had the exams just before Christmas I came third from the top of the class of 32 boys. When we had the summer Exams I came second from the top and went into 2B. At Christmas I came second again and at summer I came top of 2B so I was put into the 3A class for my third year.

About this time I joined the Bee Club in which we had to look after the bees, feeding them with a mixture of sugar and syrup in winter to keep them alive. Mr. Smith taught us how to extract the honey from the honey cones which the bees made on the frames that were put in the hive. First you had to take the smoke bellows and get some cardboard, and light it so it would smoke, and then you had to put it into the bellows and blow the smoke into the hive. The idea was that it would alarm the bees who would eat as much as they could and put them in a good mood so that they wouldn't sting you when took the top of the hive off to get the honey frame out. When that was done you took the frames, scraped the beeswax off the front and put them into the extractor to get the honey out. You put the frames into the slots, then put the top on and turned the handle so that the centrifugal force would throw the honey out so that it ran down into the bottom of the extractor. Then you could fill the jam jars which we had brought from home by undoing the tap at the bottom of the extractor so the honey would run in. We sold the jars so we could buy more sugar and things for the bees.

I also joined the Rabbit, Hen and Gardening Clubs. The hens we had were Light Suffolks which were mostly white with black speckles around their necks. They were very good layers. The cockerel was very proud about his hens and did a lot of crowing. They were allowed to roam around the garden so that they were classed as free range and most of the eggs were fertile so we would have chickens to carry on the flock. The rabbits were Black Havana and were skinned for their coats which were removed, dried out and cured and then sold to make gloves and other fur goods.

The Headmaster taught us how to kill, gut and skin the rabbits when they were big enough, but I couldn't do it because I was too scared – even though I had watched Mam dress the hens that I have already mentioned.

We all had a good laugh in the Gardening Club. The tools were kept in a shed – spades, forks, hoes and rakes, and different sizes of clogs, which people kept putting worms, caterpillars and much worse in. You had to check them before you put them on, and it was much to your own peril if you forgot!

The Headmaster ran the Gardening Club and taught us how to prune trees and how to graft fruit trees as well. He grafted a pear tree which grew one large pear which was his pride and joy. He posted prefects on watch so nobody could take it and eat it. Well, most of the school kept watching it and one day we came to school and you can imagine how he felt when he discovered somebody had eaten the pear during the night and had just left the core hanging on the tree. He never did find out who had eaten it – but it wasn't me because I lived at Lostock.

When I was in Class 3A there was an Eisteddfod at Alderley Edge and the Headmaster entered me to play my recorder, so I practised the song 'The Minstrel Boy' for about six weeks till the day came to play. When we got to Alderley Edge and saw the hall it looked very big and crowded and I got very nervous. I still played quite well but when you're competing against pianos, trumpets and violins, a recorder doesn't make much of an impression on the judges.

I used to take our Jean to the pictures on a Thursday night. We would have 2s 6d (12.5p) to go with which paid for us to get into the pictures and also covered the bus fare home. However, we usually walked home and spent the money on ice cream. I also took her on a Saturday afternoon matinee which we called the 'threepenny bug rush' because you had to queue up and wait for the cinema to open, and if you were too near the front you would get crushed up to the doors with all the people pushing to get in. We would have to stand up while 'God Save The King' was played and then settle down to watch the films. They showed serials so that you would return week after week. Usually it seemed to be about Sherlock Holmes, the detective. Then there would be a cartoon and a singalong where all the words came up on the screen – a bit like an early karaoke – and then the main picture. If you went every week you could collect points so that you could get in free at Christmas.

About this time most of the gang had started smoking and bought cigarette papers for tuppence a packet. To get the tobacco we would go 'dimping' (picking fag ends up out of the gutter) and then roll up the tobacco into cigarettes to smoke – an early form of re-cycling, I suppose! If they didn't have any money for fag papers they used to get an acorn, take the inside out, make a little pipe and fill it with tobacco, and smoke it that way. I tried it once and didn't like it, but I smoked in later life.

When we went down to Wade Brook we found that the big lads had made a rope swing across it. You had to get a branch, reach out and hook the rope, run half-way up the bank, then jump onto the knot which acted as a seat and swing across the river. When you came back across somebody else would jump on, and then other lads would jump on as well, till there were about six of us on the rope – then we would jump off on the other side of the river, one by one. We had a lot of fun messing about on the swing.

By going over the pipe bridge that went over the canal at Bucks

Field we found some big sandstone blocks stacked up which must have weighed about a ton each. They would have been used to block the roads off if the Germans had managed to get over to England during the war. After we discovered the stones we started to build dens and hideouts amongst them, and to play hide and seek and 'tick'. Across the road was the Harris Haulage and Basket Company. They made the baskets to carry the big bottles of sulphuric acid which were used for batteries. The metal was very thin and held together with steel rivets, which were good ammunition for our catapults.

There was a warehouse alongside the sandstone blocks. We found a hole in the wall and if you went in there were tins of food, peas, beans and rice pudding, which we heated up on a fire that we built in our dens. Our mothers wondered why we weren't hungry when we got home for tea.

The people who lived on Manchester Road itself used to think that they were better than those who lived down the streets. One day our mother had to put a couple right and we had bit of trouble with them. Afterwards the 'Cruelty Man' (NSPCC inspector) called Mr. Packer came to our house to see if my sister and I were being neglected or ill-treated, because somebody had reported Mam and Dad, saying that we were being abused. We were visited by Mr. Packer for a couple of months but he stopped coming when he realized we were not being ill-treated and that somebody had been telling lies to get our parents into trouble. Mam had a good idea who it was but she wouldn't say. Anyway, I can say that we were never beaten or ill-treated by our parents and were very well fed and clothed. If other children were treated as well there wouldn't be any need for Children In Need.

I remember when our Dad was on night shift and we were a bit noisy after we had come home from school, we had to go up to the bedroom to get the strap for waking him up. He would make us hold our hands out, hit us with a cloth strap and we would pretend to cry – till we got out of the bedroom. We started laughing when we got downstairs. That was the only punishment we ever got from our parents and it didn't hurt us.

There was an outbreak of Diphtheria in the village and when a few of the children caught it they had to go into the Isolation Hospital at Davenham. It was discovered that our Jean was the carrier of the germ and she was taken in as well to have her tonsils removed. I didn't catch it because I was in close contact with our Jean and therefore was immune. Someone had organized a charabanc (coach) trip to New Brighton on the Saturday when Jean was in hospital, so I asked Mam if we could go on it. She said she hadn't got any money but if I could borrow

Mam and Dad in later years

some we could go because there were two seats left. So I borrowed five shillings (25p) from Mr. Jones to pay for the tickets. When Saturday came Mam and I were very excited because we had never been to the seaside. Mam had got 2s 6d left (12.5p) for us to go with, so she made some jam butties for our dinner and we also took a bottle of barley water so we didn't have to buy a drink. We stopped at the half-way house for some refreshments but Mam and I stayed on the charabanc.

When we arrived at New Brighton we were even more excited. All of the people got off the coach and went off and left us because they knew we didn't have much money. Anyway Mam was quite happy to sit in the sun on the beach and watch me play and when I got fed up I went to help the donkey man selling rides to the children. I had to lift them on, take them up the beach on the donkeys, turn them round, then bring them back and lift them off. He let me have some free rides and he gave me 2s 6d for helping him in the morning. He told me I could help him in the afternoon if I wanted to, and I said that I would. I went and got two cups of tea and two custard tarts to go with the butties for our dinner. Mam asked where I'd got the money from and I told her from the man on the donkeys that I had been helping and that I was going to help him in the afternoon. So we had a good dinner of the tea, butties and custards. Soon after we'd had dinner some of the people on the trip came and told us that they hadn't had any dinner because all the cafés had been full. Mam and I had a good laugh about it because they again thought they were better than us and didn't want to know us. But we'd the last laugh. When the lads found out what I had been doing they wanted to help and so I asked the donkey man if it was all right and he said 'yes'. I let them do the work while I collected the money. At the end of the afternoon the man said we had done very well and gave me a ten-shilling note (50p) so I got it changed for four half-crowns, gave the lads 2s 6d each and kept five shillings for myself. When we got back on the coach to come back home Mam started to sing, everybody joined in and after that everyone enjoyed themselves. It was my first time at the seaside and a most enjoyable day. The best part about it was that I paid Mr Jones the five shillings back that I had borrowed.

At the hospital they had found that the Diphtheria germ was in an abscess on our Jean's neck. When they removed it she was all right and was allowed home.

When you went over the canal bridge along Manchester Road you came to Griffiths Road which was also known as 'Charlie's back lane'. I never found out why it was called that. Along the road you would go past J.W. Barrow's – which was a road haulage company were I worked as garage foreman years later – and then under the railway bridge. The height of the bridge at the time was 13ft 6in but over the years it has reduced to 12ft. It hasn't gone lower but the build-up of tarmac over the years has made the road higher than it was. Next was Harris Transport where I also worked in later life. Further down towards Rudheath was Wade Brook which ran under the road and through I.C.I., and then Watson's Farm in the hollow. Mr and Mrs Watson used to deliver milk around the village with a pony and trap and you had to take a jug to get the milk because there weren't any milk bottles – they came years later. You had to say how much you wanted – such as a gill, half a pint, a pint or a quart – and they would put the milk in the jug and mark it down in their book. We paid for the milk at the weekend when Dad got his wages. Further down the road were the lime beds where we went to get Peewit eggs in spring. We also used to get Sand Martins' and Kingfishers' eggs along the sand banks on the River Eye. My mate Tom would break the birds' eggs into his hand and then eat them raw. Across the road from the lime beds was I.C.I and then a footbridge over the canal tow path back to Works Lane. But when you went back along Griffiths Road towards Lostock you passed the stack of big sandstone blocks that I have already mentioned and the warehouse. Alongside the warehouse was a black and white cottage where the Langstons lived. It was knocked down after the war. After the cottage was the railway, then under the bridge was wasteland and Renalds & Bodens car body and spray garage.

Mrs Jones, Tom's mam, gave us some old pram wheels and we made a 'plank-a-bus' with them. We got a plank of wood and fastened the axles to it. We made the one at the back rigid so it wouldn't turn and then we fixed the front one in the middle so we could steer it with our feet or with a piece of rope – and we fitted a wooden box as a seat. We took it in turns, one pulling or one pushing and one riding and we also used to jump on and go downhill on it.

Tom and I got a job working at Fryer's Farm at nights and on a Saturday. To get to the farm from our house we went up Manchester Road, over the canal bridge and down through a field to Hall Lane, then on to Green Lane and turned right into the farm. It was quite a large farm for the time, about 250 acres, with a big herd of cows and also two Shires which did all the carting and ploughing, and all the work that needed horse power. Tractors were a bit dear at the time so horses did most of the work.

The farmhouse had some windows that had been bricked up and painted to look like windows. Apparently it was because of a Window Tax in the olden days – people bricked their windows up so they wouldn't have to pay tax on them. The farm was built in the form of a square with the house and garden and then the pigsties, the cowshed (shippon) and then the stable. I could never understand why the pigsties were nearest the house.

When there weren't any potatoes to pick or harvesting to be done, or when it was raining, we helped the farm workers to clean out and whitewash the pigsties and the stable (I don't remember white-washing the shippon) and collect the eggs from around the farm and take them to Mrs Fryer at the house.

When springtime came we started to plant potatoes and we found the work very hard because we weren't very big. We worked with three men who carried two split boxes and we lads worked in the middle, so between us we did five drills at a time. When we got bigger we carried a split box between us and did two drills. One day when Tom and I were planting potatoes it started to rain but we decided to finish the potatoes that were left on the trailer. When we got down to the last split box Mr Fryer brought another trailer load in the field, so we tied potato sacks around our waists like an apron to keep our knees dry. We used another bag to form a hood to keep our heads and backs dry. By this time it had started to rain very heavily and we agreed it was too wet to carry on. We decided to go home because we were soaked. We didn't go back for a few days and Mr Fryer called to see what the trouble was. We told him we thought he had been too harsh expecting us to work in all that rain and that we had got another job. He said that he would pay us for that day and give us a pay rise if we carried on working for him, and said he realized that we were lads not men.

We liked potato-picking time because Harry, the man who looked after the horses, would let us go and bring them up from the field and help him to harness them so they could pull the potato digger. When the digger had thrown the potatoes out of the drill we picked them up and put them in a big basket, called a hamper, which held about a hundredweight of potatoes. When it was full we would shute them into a potato sack and then they were loaded onto the cart and taken up to the farm where they were weighed properly, tied up with string and put ready to be sent to the potato merchant. At dinner time we went up to the farm to feed the horses and also have our meal in the stable. Sometimes Harry would let us take in turns to feed the horses.

The horses were called Sammy and Smiler and they were both crossbred Shires. Sam was brown with a black mane and tail and was quite well behaved but cold-blooded. Smiler was different again, still calm and the same height as Sam, but he had a wicked sense of humour and a small beard that gave the impression that he was laughing at you. When we fed the horses we gave them four scoops of feed each and I am sure that Smiler could count because when you went up between the horses to put the feed in the trough he always knew when you took the last scoop because he would move over to hem you in and you would have to go under his belly to get out – then he would turn round and look at you as though he was laughing at you. As I have said they were very gentle and wouldn't hurt you on purpose.

After we had planted the potatoes Harry would come along with the driller and cover the potatoes up so they would grow and when they had grown up through the soil they were drilled up again to keep the frost from killing them. Then it was hay-time when the grass was cut with a mowing machine that laid the stalks out in neat rows. When the grass was dry on one side we turned it over with pikeles so the other side could dry as well. When it was completely dry we knocked it into small piles of hay and then loaded it on to the hay carts to take it to the haystacks that were built in the corner of the field. The grass had to be very dry because if it was stacked up wet it could set on fire.

When were about thirteen years old we were classed as 'nearly big lads' and we could help the bigger lads to get the trees for the November 5th bonfire. We cut down hawthorn, elderberry and willow trees that all burned quite well. We would pull the trees back to the Tip Bonk and make a bonfire to be ready for Bonfire Night. At night after school we would have to guard the bonfire in case a rival gang from the Smut Bonk decided to pinch our trees. Some of us would go around the houses ('souling') begging for money for fireworks. We used to sing:

"This night we come a-souling, a-souling this night,
"If you haven't got a penny a half penny will do,
"If you haven't got a half penny – God Bless You!"

We usually got a bit of money given to us, not for the singing but so we would go away!

One Bonfire Night one of the boys had a lot of fireworks. He wouldn't share them with anybody and wouldn't even let anyone have the empty cases from the used fireworks. He kept putting the used cases in his left hand pocket and he had the unused ones in his right-hand pocket. We told him not to do that in case he made a mistake but as usual he didn't take any notice, being so clever. But he wasn't so clever when he did make a mistake and put a case in his right-hand pocket which set the others alight. He had to go to hospital with a badly burnt leg and was in there for four weeks.

We used to make a den in the middle of the bonfire so the Smuts couldn't see us but we could see them and chase them away, because we usually made the biggest fire. On November 5th we would take the fire to pieces to make sure that nobody was still in the den. We would then get any old paper or anything else that would start the fire going quickly, rebuild the bonfire and put the Guy Fawkes on top that someone had made to get money for their fireworks by begging "A penny for the Guy". We would then wait till it had got dark at about 6.30pm and light the bonfire at about 7 o'clock. When the fire got really going we would get a garden spade and clear the bottom cupboard out of all the old newspapers and cockroaches, as I said before. When the fire had burnt down to red embers we would put potatoes in the embers and have baked potatoes which we ate with a bit of margarine and salt. After everybody had gone home we would stoke up the fire so it would be still alight next morning.

One day Mam went round to see Mrs Jones for a 'cant' (a talk to catch up with the local gossip) and found she was just going to drink a bottle of disinfectant because she said later that she was fed up with life and wanted to die. Mam stopped her and after that they became very good friends. We had a good laugh one day. Mam went round to see Mrs Jones, who had told her that she was on a diet to lose some weight. But when Mam got there her friend was eating a large plate of potatoes, carrots, cabbage, meat and gravy and when Mam asked her about the diet she said that she had eaten the diet and now she was having her dinner.

Our Mam got me a Saturday job at Lord's butcher's shop delivering meat and scrubbing out the boxes that the meat was put in before being loaded on to the vans ready for delivery. I delivered the meat out of a basket which was fitted to the front of the bicycle in a carrier. The bike had a small wheel at the front and a big wheel at the back. When the basket was full of meat I couldn't ride the bike because it was very heavy, so I had to wait till I had delivered half the meat then I could ride it to finish off the first delivery which was down most of the streets. I had to return to the shop for the second delivery which was down as far as Cranage and then I had to go back to the shop and scrub the blood off the meat boxes ready for Mrs. Lord to inspect them – and if they weren't clean enough I had to do them again. For four hours' work on the Saturday I got five shillings (25p). One Saturday it was very frosty and when I went out on the bike with a full basket of meat the front wheel slipped on the ice and all the meat fell out of the basket all over the road. After I had picked it up I had to go back to the shop where it was washed off and rewrapped so I could deliver it. Mrs. Lord wasn't very pleased and I think she would have sacked me but for the fact that she was a friend of Mam's. I found out later that they had been in service together.

When I got the job at Lord's, Mam said that I could have a new bike so she took me down to Jack Gee's bike shop where she signed for it on hire purchase and paid £1 deposit. I had to pay five shillings a week for it and so I had to keep my job at Lord's until it was paid for. It was a Phillips drop-handlebar red racing bike. I used to clean it and oil it and look after it very well.

At school I had gone into 4 Rural class because I wanted to go into agriculture when I left school. We were allowed to go farming in the afternoons so the school arranged for us to work for Mr J Ford's farm at Arley. Mr Ford had two sons, Joe who was the elder and Peter who was the younger. Pete was only about four years older than us and he used to let us get the horses ready with him so we could get potatoes. Mr Ford or one of his sons would pick us up in their car, a Humber Super Snipe, from school after dinner so we could work on the farm and when we had finished would return us back to school. But Tom and I stayed faithful to Mr Fryer at weekends and during the school holidays because we knew the farm and the farm workers and he paid us a bit more than we would get anywhere else, because we had been with him for a few years. We also knew and liked the two horses.

We liked harvest time, best of all following the binder, and were amazed how it would cut and tie the corn into bundles so we could collect them and stack them into stooks – which was eight bundles on the bottom, four either side and eight on the top. When the corn was dry we loaded it onto the carts, took it up to the farm and stacked it into the Dutch barns which looked like black sheds on stilts. The corn was allowed to dry and the next phase was the thrashing which was done by the thrasher.

It was quite a big occasion when the thrashing machine came and it was set up in the farmyard with the tractor – usually a Field Marshal – which powered the thrasher and the baler. First in line there was the tractor, then the thrasher and then the baler. The corn was fed into the thrasher and then was separated from the straw and chaff. The corn was put into bags, the chaff was put into other bags and the straw was baled. We usually got the job of carrying the chaff to the midden – the manure heap. The bales of straw were then stacked back into the Dutch barn. The corn was taken up to be stored into the 'bing'. It was a very dirty and noisy job, was thrashing, but when it was finished a great feeling of achievement was experienced by all and it was a time of celebration for a successful harvest gathered in.

After the harvest we would start preparing for winter. We had to get the turnips in ready to feed the cows when they were brought in for winter. We had to 'top and tail' them (cut the roots and leaves off), load them on to the carts, take them to the farm and put them into a 'hog' which was a shallow pit that had been dug so they could be stacked up, covered with straw and would keep till they were needed for cattle feed.

About this time of the year when there wasn't much to do we had to go hedging and ditching (clearing out the ditches and cutting the hedges) and whitewashing the shippons and stables out so they looked nice and clean ready for the new year.

Now that I had got my bike I started to go to see Aunty Alice who was our dad's sister and lived at Mobberley with her children (Jimmy, Joyce, Dorothy, Nellie, Kenneth, Roy and Trevor). Our Uncle Jimmy had been killed in a road accident one foggy day in 1947 on his way to work on his motor bike. He hit a lorry that had parked without any parking lights on. I rode to see them most weekends and used to go for a week's holiday in the summer. Young Jimmy worked on Spibie's Farm which had horses as well as being a mixed farm, so I enjoyed working there as well.

Dad's brother Uncle Wilf had given Dad an Alsatian dog called Judy but what he didn't tell us that she was having pups. We had only had her about six weeks when she had two pups, one which I called Rustler who was black, tan and white, and the other one, Prince, who was all black. Judy must have picked up some poison because she wouldn't let the pups feed from her, she wouldn't eat and would only drink water. One day she left home and I went to look for her. I found her dead down by the Water Works, so I went home for a spade and buried her on common land which I had been told was within the law.

Mam decided to have the pups' tails docked because the people who wanted Prince preferred him to have a short tail, and so we asked Mr. Trayner to come and do it for us. He came to our house, picked up Rustler, bit half his tail off and spat it into a bucket and then did the same to Prince.

We had to hand-rear both of the pups till they were old enough to eat by themselves and Mam and Dad decided to keep Rustler, who grew into a big dog. He was also very clever and didn't need much training. He seemed to understand everything you said to him and I spent a lot of time with him. I used to take him all over the fields and across the canal to Marbury Woods and Forge Pool, where he liked to swim and chase the wildlife in and around the pool. I often took him out at night when it was thundering and lightning – we would stand on the bridge over the waterfall, watching the lightning bounce off the water and rolling around the sky, and the wind blowing the clouds about. It made me realize what a wonderful world we live in.

Our dad had been talking with his sister Aunty Grace about their inheritance and because Dad was the oldest son it was felt that he should enquire about it. Apparently his grandfather, our great-grandfather, had owned a soap factory in Dukinfield, Cheshire and years later we were told that he had found the formulae for Daz, Omo and 'soft soap', which was used to help launch ships at shipyards up and down the country. When the soft soap, which looked like brown grease, was smeared on to the slipways at the shipyards it was very slippery and the ships would be launched quite easily.

Our granddad was the oldest of two sons, his name was Wilfred Ernest Bray Mellor, the 'Bray' being his mother's maiden name which was usually given to the oldest son. His brother's name was Hubert and Dad knew him as Uncle Hugh. With Granddad being the oldest son it made him the heir so that he would eventually inherit the business when his dad died. Our granddad had had a private education and had been to Cambridge until he had run away to sea. Mam told us he could speak French and German, knew Latin and could play the piano like a concert pianist. Well, his father found him a year later and brought him home to learn the business. He stayed at home for about a year and decided to do his own thing so he ran away again and joined The Royal Horse Artillery. This time his father disinherited him and passed the business over to his younger brother, Hugh. Dad and I went to a big house in Dukinfield to see Uncle Hugh and when we went to the front door and rang the bell it was answered by a maid. Dad said who we were and she told us to go round to the back door, so we did and we had to wait in the kitchen till Uncle Hugh came to see us. When he came he was quite pleasant and the maid brought us some tea and scones which we had with Uncle Hugh. I can remember being very embarrassed about the whole thing because I felt that we were imposing – I got the impression that he thought that we were after something, which I wasn't and I had only gone with Dad because he had insisted.

I was still in the Scouts and had risen to Patrol Leader of the Woodpecker Patrol. I think that I only got it because I was due to go into the Senior Scouts and it would be my last camp in Dyseth in North Wales where we usually went for a week. The Scout Camp was a big occasion and on the Saturday we had to assemble at the Scout Hall for 8am to load up the lorry which was to take us to the camp in Wales. When we got to the field in Wales the first task was to unload the lorry so that it could return to Lostock. Then we raced each other to see who could get their tent up first. We cleared a place for the camp fire and cooking area, and tried to get out of digging the latrines – the job every body disliked. When the camp was ready we had tea and were allowed to go into Rhyl as long as we were back for 10pm.

Most of us enjoyed the camp very much because it was usually our only holiday away from home. We cooked our meals over the camp fire which made the food taste of woodsmoke because all we could burn was wood collected from the hedgerows and the nearby wood. In the evening we would play games, most of which I have already mentioned, and we also went out after midnight to do some night tracking when one patrol had to go out and lay a trail and the another patrol had to follow by reading the clues. There was also a 'Ghost Night' in Rhyl, when everybody dressed up as ghosts and went around town scaring people. Now I suppose we know it as Hallowe'en, so I think we had it long before the Americans ever had 'Trick or Treat'.

Bricks, brews and Mr Breeze

One day when I was talking to Mam she asked me what I was going to do when I left school. I said that I was going farming because I had been interested in working on a farm since I was a young boy. But she told me that farm workers' wages were very poor and the only people who got rich on a farm were the owners – I would never be able to afford to buy a farm, she said. Mam advised that I would be better off learning a trade and so I decided to be a motor mechanic. I hoped that I wouldn't have to do shift-work like Dad did. Dad had left the British Octel Company after the war had finished and had got a job at I.C.I. Lostock, so I went for a job there too when I left school at 15 years old.

I had to start at I.C.I. Winnington Works, Northwich. The hours we worked were from 8am till 5pm with an hour for dinner for five days a week. We were employed in a section called General Services which meant all the labouring jobs were done by our gang. We looked after the gardens, weeding, digging and maintaining the lawns and hedges as well as keeping the Works tidy. Once a week we had to clean out the canteen floor. We moved out all the tables and chairs, brushed the floor, scrubbed it with soap and hot water and swilled it out with cold water. We would then use squeegees to dry the floor and when it was dry enough we had to set to and polish with big polishers and then use bumpers to get the final shine on the surface. And after it was done we would put all the tables and chairs back.

When I had been there about a fortnight I was transferred to the Brick Gang whose job was to unload the bricks from the railway wagons and stack them into the different types and grades of bricks. It was very hard work. We worked from 7.30am till 10am and stopped for 10 minutes for a drink of cocoa and a new pair of work gloves. Then it was back to work till 12 noon when we had a one-hour break for dinner which was served in the canteen. The dinner ladies usually gave us young lads big helpings, and we didn't have any trouble eating them because we worked so hard. After dinner we played football for half an hour and then we went back to the Brick Fields to unload more wagons till 3pm. We had another 10-minute break for a mug of tea and we finished for the day at 5.30pm.

We had to unload the rail wagons by hand and formed a chain so that each person did not have to throw the bricks too far. There were two lads in the wagon who put the bricks onto a roller and then two others at the bottom of the roller who would take the bricks off and throw them to the first lads in the chain. They then passed them along till the bricks had got to where they were being stored and the last two lads stacked them. We would take turns at unloading, passing and stacking the bricks and it hurt if you got your thumbs in between the bricks as you caught them to put on the stack. You soon learned to move your thumbs out of the way. At the end of the day we were allowed to have a wash because we were covered in brick dust and during a single day's work we would have worn out four pairs of gloves. For a week's work we received £2 2s 0d.

At this time I left the Scouts and joined the Boys' Club which was held in the games room at the Scout Hall. We could still have a bath there. We had a snooker table, table tennis, a dart board and a hoop board. We learned to play all the games and I found that I liked snooker best. Everybody seemed to be growing bigger than me and some lads thought that they could bully me. But what they didn't realise was that with all the farming that I'd been doing, and delivering meat on Saturday, I was fairly strong for my size – as one or two found out. I remember one boy named Tommy who was a lot bigger and was trying to show off to his mates. He wanted to fight me but I said that I had come to play games and didn't want to fight anybody because I didn't have anything to prove. As always, he insisted, so when I had given him a good hiding he got his mates on to me. I was frightened and started to run up Works Lane, but one of his friends was a better runner than me and I knew that he would catch me. My brain went into gear and I thought that if I stopped suddenly when he had nearly caught me up, bent down and braced myself, he would go flying over the top of me. That is what I did and it worked. When he landed there wasn't much fight left in him and when the other lad saw what had happened he decided that he wasn't having any of that so he went back. I went home quite pleased and the next time I saw them they weren't so clever. We all shook hands and became good mates.

When I had been at I.C.I. about two months we had to take a Trade Test to get into the Vocational School that was run by the company to pick out the people that they wanted to be tradesmen. The Trade Test consisted of a written test and a practical test. The written test was on general subjects and the practical test was to see if you could co-ordinate your hands and mind. You had to pick up a ball bearing out of a box with your left hand, put it into a little shute, watch it go up and across and then down the other side, then you would pick it up with your right hand and put it back into the box on the left hand side and see how many you could do in one minute. After that you went into another room and on the bench where there was an electric light bulb holder, a back door lock, a toilet chain and a bicycle bell which were all in pieces and you had to put them together in five minutes so that they all worked. Being mechanically-minded, I found that test quite easy. After about a week we got the results and I am happy to say that I got into the Vocational School.

I started about a week after I got the results and I was very glad to get off the Brick Gang. The first day at the school we were introduced to the routine and were divided up into classes. We worked from 8am to 4.30pm and the day started with Physical Training. Afterwards we had a shower which made me a bit embarrassed because most of the lads were bigger than me and had hairy chests. I only had very fine hair – because I was a bit late developing. After the shower we went to our classes. We did six weeks at the following subjects: fitting, boiler-making, woodwork, plumbing, electrics, brick laying and chemistry. After the six weeks we had a test and then moved onto the next subject till we had done all the different trades, the idea being that you became an apprentice to the one you were best at. My best subject was chemistry.

Just before Christmas we had a party and we were asked if we could do any party pieces. I gave a turn on my recorder, starting with "God Save The King" and they all stood up. I played some carols and other tunes that I knew and then finished off with the National Anthem so they would all stand up again like a standing ovation.

After Christmas Dr. Muir Smith, the head teacher, called us in to tell us what trade we were going to do and when I went in to see him he said that I had done very well at chemistry and that was what I would be doing at I.C.I. – because after all it was a chemical company and that was my going to be my job. But as soon as he mentioned shift work I knew that I still wanted to be a mechanic so I put my notice in to leave. All hell broke loose and Dr. Smith sent for Dad to come from Lostock Works to have a word with me and persuade me to change my mind and take the job that was offered which had a bright future. I found out afterwards that Dr. Smith had sent a car to collect my dad so he could talk me round into staying. That night when Dad came home he got on to me about staying on and what a good career I would have and by the end of the night he had convinced me. I went into work next day and withdrew my notice and I must say that Dr Smith was very pleased. But he wasn't very pleased the next day when I went in and put my notice in again and so I left I.C.I..

I didn't have a job to go to but there were plenty about at that time, so I got on my bike and found work at Pimlotts boatyard heating rivets till there was a vacancy for an apprentice fitter. After about two months a job came up but then they told me that I wasn't old enough because I wasn't 16, and so I left. I was rather sorry to leave, really, because I was getting interested in marine engines. They built a large variety of boats, like sea-going tugs and coasters, and while I was there they were constructing two aluminium launches for the Canadian Government to ferry scientists across the Great Lakes. When you went on board and down into the cabins it was like going into a bus, with seats on either side, a gangway in the middle and a lot of windows down each side. They were powered by two Rolls-Royce engines. But I couldn't bear the prospect of heating rivets till I was 16.

I tried all the local garages but they hadn't any vacancies. I was on the verge of giving up when I was cycling past an entry and noticed a lot of cars down at the bottom. I rode down to see and found there was a garage in an old foundry. I went up to a man in overalls and asked if there were any vacancies and was the boss about? He said that he was the boss and then he asked me why I wanted to be a mechanic. I said that I thought that it was an interesting job as there must be lots of different things to do on so many makes of cars and lorries. Anyway he said that the first 25 years were the worse, but if I was still interested I could start at 8 am on Monday. And so I started work for Mr. Harry Breeze at the Foundry Garage, Vearows Place, London Road, Leftwich.

As I was the youngest I was the 'gofer' which meant that I had to do all the menial jobs like making the tea at brew time and brushing out the garage twice a day. Mr Breeze started to call me by the nickname 'Shirty' and when I asked him why he said that he always gave his young lads a nickname and being that as I wasn't very big it suited me. No matter what people say about how I got the nickname, that was how I got it.

When I made the tea at brew time ('baggin' time), I had to put the kettle on to boil and while it was getting hot I got the teapot and cups ready. When the kettle had boiled I brewed the tea and had to pour into the cups – remembering who had milk and sugar and who didn't. At 9.55am I had to stand by the time clock and blow the whistle so the lads would know that it was brew time. I had to stand by the clock till 10am and then blow the whistle again to let them know that brew time was over. Then I could have my own tea while I was washing the pots up ready for the afternoon break when I did the same thing all over again. After I had finished with the pots I had to help the mechanics and also work with Mr. Breeze. At last I felt that I was learning a trade.

We had to repair all makes of cars, doing overhauls on engines, gearboxes, clutches, road-springs and rear axles, as well as brake re-lines and bodywork respraying. Being the youngest lad I was still doing most of the menial jobs and one day while I was working with Mr Breeze he told me how I could get promoted and get out of brewing the tea because now and again he gave the lads a test by giving them the same type of job to do and the loser of the test was demoted to tea lad. The job we had to do in the test was to strip all the paint off a 1938 Morris 10hp down to the bare metal and when we had done that we had to clean off the rust till all the bodywork was clean. The winner would be promoted to work mostly with Mr. Breeze. He drew a chalk line down the middle of the car and we had to do one side each. First he showed us what to do and I listened to what he said. I won and I started to work with Mr. Breeze as his apprentice.

The first thing I learned was how to service a car, starting with checking the engine, gearbox, axle and steering box for oil and topping them up using the right grade of oil if it was below the mark on the dipstick. Then we had to clean and oil all the grease nipples (which made us laugh when the word 'nipple' was used) and know where to look to find them. We also had to check the vehicle over for loose bolts and anything that was liable to drop off, and to repair anything that we found wrong. We put the work we had done on the job sheet so that the customer could be charged. We also had to oil all the door and boot locks and catches, tighten the wheelnuts and blow the tyres up to the correct pressure – including the spare wheel. We were given one hour to do all this.

I worked with Mr. Breeze quite a lot and he taught me gas welding, soldering, brazing and leading which was used when repairing the bodywork and the wings (mudguards). When there was a hole in a wing you had to repair it. First you had to cut out all of the rust, make a patch to go into the hole and weld it in, fill the patch up with lead and smooth it down to the shape of the wing with a rasp, and then finally fill it with stopping ready for painting.

Mr. Breeze was very strict about all the work that was undertaken and you had to do all the repairs to the best of your ability. If you didn't know how to do them and you got stuck you were expected to ask him how to do the job instead of trying to do what you didn't know. He would come and show you and that was the way we were taught. I enjoyed working with Mr. Breeze and learned a lot from him. One of his favourite tricks was to stop an engine from running by shorting out the plug leads with his fingers. He showed me how, but I wasn't brave enough to do it. I could however hold one of the plug leads while the engine was running: the secret was to hold the plug lead as tight as you could and then all you felt was a slight tingling in your wrist which didn't hurt – until someone touched the car and then you got a shock which made you jump! There was about 18,000 volts at the plugs but the amperage was very small and that it was the amperage that caused the trouble.

Now and again Mr. Breeze used to try our common sense by asking us to do things, such as sending us to the ironmongers for pigeon milk, a sky hook, a big weight, and a long stand – to name but a few. He must have been talking to Mr. Weston the ironmonger because he knew what to do and say when you went into the shop. I'm glad to say that he didn't catch me out.

I got demoted back to 'can lad' because I picked up a brush to clean out the garage and as I was brushing the head of the brush broke in two pieces so I put it by the bench and got another one. But someone put it under the bench and when Mr. Breeze found it he wanted to know who had broken it. He got us altogether and asked who had done it and when I admitted it was me he clouted me across the ear and knocked me over. Although it hurt I was determined I wouldn't cry even though I was only 16 years old. Anyway he demoted me, so I had to start again from the bottom and was 'can lad' again.

When the weather got cold I had to light a brazier, a 40-gallon drum with holes in it which stood on house bricks. To light it you put paper and sticks in and coke on top, then poured paraffin over it and set it alight. This was the only heating we had in the big building and if you felt cold you were told to work harder. When the brazier was burning well we got some water in a bucket and put it alongside to warm so we could rinse our hands off with soap after we had got most off the dirt off in paraffin.

There was a furnace under the sprayshop that heated it up so that it was hot when Mr. Breeze was spraying a car. When we ran out of coke I had to get a four-wheeled pull truck and six hessian two-hundredweight bags, draw 15 shillings from the office, and then go to the gasworks to fill the bags up with coke.

When you were the 'can lad' you also had to go and collect parts from the bus and railway stations but mostly from Old Hartford station. You had to use your own bike and the journey there and back was about six miles which took about 20 minutes. I broke the record and did it in 15 minutes and so I got promoted back to work with Mr. Breeze which made me very happy because there were some engines to overhaul.

Mr. Breeze didn't pay overtime but if you wanted to you could do jobs at night 'on contract'. I used to get £3 for helping him at night. We would send the engine block to Willhall Engineering Company, who would rebore it, fit new pistons and regrind the crankshaft. When we got the engine block back I had to wash it off with Gunk, leave the Gunk soaking for about half an hour, wash the Gunk off with water and then blow all the water off with the high pressure airline, making sure that all the swarf was washed out so it didn't block the oilways and galleries up. Next I had to take the engine block into the fitting shop ready to be built up to the complete engine. After I had done that I had to wash off all the other parts ready for fitting: the oil pump, sump, timing cover, cylinder-head, clutch assembly and flywheel. And then I had to get all the correct nuts and bolts, the correct spanners and a new clutch plate and gaskets. Mr. Breeze said that doing all this would teach me and get me used to the different spanner sizes (British Standard Whitworth, British Standard Fine, American National Fine and the metric sizes) and which threads were used on what kind of engine. When it was ready for Mr. Breeze to come and build up the engine I would then go home for my tea and when I returned Mr. Breeze would be in the shop ready to start. He usually fitted the oil pump first and then the sump filter and the sump and then turned the engine over on to the sump and blocked the engine up so that it was safe to work on. Next he would fit the camshaft (a shaft that had cams on it to open the valves in sequence). He would fit the flywheel and then turn the crankshaft so that number 1 and number 4 pistons were at T.D.C. (top dead centre) so he could time the engine up to start up when it was fitted in the car. He would check in the book that told how many degrees before T.D.C. the inlet valve opened so that you could work out how much you had to turn the flywheel back before fitting the timing chain and putting timing marks on the timing gears.

We only had one light on in the fitting shop at night and if I had forgotten something and had to go and get it from the bench at the other end of the garage I was allowed to switch one more light on so that I could see to go across the pit. If I forgot to switch it off when I came back there was a talk about how much electricity cost and how I must make sure that I switched it off in future.

Mr. Breeze would allow half a pint of petrol to wash the dynamo and starter motor off because with them being electrical components paraffin would take too long to dry.

In 1950 I worked on my first new car which was a Vauxhall L model. It had been on the road for about six weeks while we were waiting for some new stuff called 'underseal' to come to protect the underneath of the car. It was like a red rubbery mixture that gave off a heavy petroleum vapour. Mr. Breeze asked me to do the car on contract at night and so I said that I would do it for £5. He agreed and put the car over the pit.

First of all I had to clean off six weeks' worth of road dirt with a wire brush and petrol on cotton wool so that the underseal would stick to the underneath of the car. The underseal was put into a pressure container, given a good stirring so that it was well mixed, the lid was put on and screwed down with four wing bolts and then I connected the airline and adjusted the pressure to 80psi (pounds per square inch). The underseal came up a thick pipe to the spray-gun and came out in a fine spray so that you could spray the underneath of the car. Before you could start spraying you had to mask the paint off with newspaper so that you didn't get any underseal on the bodywork.

The pit was about six feet deep and being little I had to stand on a wooden box so that I could reach into all the corners. It took me about two hours to spray the underneath because it had to be done properly and if I had missed any I would only have had to do it again. After I had finished I felt very funny and was seeing double. Mr. Breeze said that I was drunk on the fumes so he put my head between my legs and started to pump me up and down to get the fumes out of my lungs. He also made me run up and down the street, and after about 10 minutes I felt a lot better. But then I had to wash the underseal off my face with petrol so I started to feel drunk again, and I had to run up and down once more before I could ride my bike home.

The next night I had to jack the car up, put it on axle stands and take the wheels off so that I could underseal underneath the wings. When I had finished, put the wheels back on and tightened up the wheelnuts I had to get somebody to check that the wheelnuts were tight. We all had to do this so that we had a witness to say that they were tight in case the wheel came loose when the car went out. I was glad when I had completed the job and tidied up, and could tell Mr. Breeze that I had finished. I was very happy to get the £5 in my wage packet on the Friday and I gave it to Mam.

One day when I came back to work after dinner as I clocked on I noticed a fire in the sprayshop. All the newspapers were on fire near the celluose and celluose thinners, which were highly inflammable, and there was a car in the spray shop. So I went to the water tap, filled up two buckets with water and started to put the fire out. It took six buckets to extinguish it completely. At first Mr. Breeze thought that I had started the fire but his dad, whom we all called 'Pop' and who was the handyman, had seen what had happened and said it had been a brave thing for me to do, saving the spray shop and more importantly the customer's car. Mr. Breeze called me into the office and said that I would get a reward for putting the fire out. In my next wage packet there was a white £5 pound note which was the first one that I had ever seen, never mind having one of my own. I gave it to Mam, too.

On a Monday once a month Mr. Breeze had to take his wife to the Asthma Clinic in Manchester for treatment so he left the senior man in charge. We used to finish all the work, then get an oilcan or a grease-gun, pick two sides and have an oil-can fight. Afterwards we had to clean off all the cars ready for the next day. I think Mr. Breeze wondered why the cars were so clean on a Tuesday.

One day when Mr. Breeze went out the senior man came to me and told me that I had to get Mr Breeze's car into the garage and service it, so I got into it, started it up and put it into reverse gear which I knew how to do because I been watching. When I let the clutch out the car started to jump backwards just as Mr. Breeze came back and caught me. I was very frightened when he opened the car door and asked me what I was doing. I told him what I had been asked to do, so he understood what had happened and said that it was about time that I learned to drive, anyway, and that if I stayed behind that night after I clocked off he would teach me. He sat in the car with me, told me what to do and let me drive in and out of the garage and around the car park in first gear until I got used to it. When I could drive fairly well he taught me how to change gear, but said that I should use only first or second gear around the garage. The next night he taught me how to ride his motorbike, a 350cc Velocette, up and down the private drive to the garage and the car park. I practised every night for a month and by that time I was fairly good so he let me start driving cars in and out of the garage. It was ironic that the mechanic who'd tried to get me into trouble actually did me a favour.

One Monday night about 6pm I felt very hungry and had to go home for my tea. As I rode my bike back I only fancied cheese, which I didn't normally like. When I got home and asked Mam for a cheese butty (sandwich) she said: "You don't like cheese!" Anyway she made me one, which to her amazement I ate, and I have loved cheese ever since.

As I have said before, the garage was very big and there was plenty of room to park old cars which we used for spares if we were stuck for parts to put our customers' cars back on the road. The war hadn't been over long and spare parts were still hard to get hold of. At the far end we kept stage scenery belonging to the Denville Players Theatre Company which put on plays and drama at The Pavilion. Mr C Denville, who owned the Players, was one of our customers. I think perhaps he liked a drink because he kept bringing his car in for body repairs such as bent bumpers, mudguards and running boards – which you don't have on modern cars – and it was good for business. When he brought his car in he was usually swaying about and when you asked him what had happened he always said that it wasn't his fault because the walls and trees kept jumping out in front of him when he passed. He was a fine actor.

One day Mr. Breeze said that we were going to make some road springs. I had to go and light the forge so that we could heat up the springs and get some old engine oil to re-temper the spring leaves when we had set them up to the correct bow or arch. As I wasn't very tall I had to stand on a box so that I could swing the sledge hammer and hit the anvil. We would take the road spring to pieces and replace the broken spring leaves – sometimes we had to make leaves out of old springs and had to cut many spring leaves to the correct length. When we had to make one we would measure the broken leaf, mark out the leaf that we were going to use and put into the forge to heat it up till it was white hot. Mr. Breeze would hold the cold chisel on the line and I would have to hit the chisel with the sledge hammer to cut the spring leaf to the correct size. Then we had to set the bow to the same as the other leaves in the spring. We had to temper the new leaf by putting it into the forge till it was cherry red, plunge it into the old engine oil to re-temper the leaf and then build the spring up ready to be fitted back onto the car.

One day when we were cutting a spring leaf, Mr. Breeze was holding the chisel and as I was about to hit it the box that I was standing on moved and the sledge hammer hit Mr. Breeze on the hand. I was expecting a clout around the ear again for hitting his hand but he said that it was his fault because he hadn't given me time to set the box up so that I could use the hammer. But, he said, I was not to miss again: I took that as a warning and I didn't! I was secretly rather glad that I had hurt his hand and thought that it was pay-back for him hitting me over the breaking of the brush that hadn't been my fault anyway – but I never told anybody what I thought.

Mr. Breeze also started to let me do some jobs on my own to see how much I had learned.

One day he said that I had worked very hard and as a reward he was going to take me to the British Industrial Fair. The event was being held in Birmingham so he decided to go on his motor bike because it would be cheaper on petrol and we would be able to weave in and out of the traffic. We had a good and interesting day out looking at all the machinery and up-to-date tools and equipment. I had a very enjoyable time both going and coming back, looking at the countryside, although it was a bit cold returning in the evening.

Mr Breeze decided that I should learn about tyres and so he transferred me to his tyre depot in London Road, next door to the Regal Cinema. Mr Joe Salisbury was the boss and he said that I could call him 'Joe'. He was a very good man at his job and what he didn't know about tyres wasn't worth knowing. He taught me how to change tyres, fit new ones and mend punctures. He also taught me how to serve petrol and take the petrol pump readings for petrol deliveries. We had to be very polite to customers and never argue with them, whether they were right or wrong, and to make sure that we served them to the best of our ability and gave them the correct change.

The hardest work was changing lorry and tractor tyres. When you changed a lorry tyre the most difficult part was removing the old tyre from the wheel. You had to let all the air out first, remove the spilt ring and the collar to expose one side of the tyre, soak the rim and tyre with soapy water and then turn the wheel over and knock the tyre off. Usually it was stuck to the rim with rust and then the hard work began, because you had to knock it off with wedges and a sledge hammer. Next you had to knock off all the rust from the wheel rim and clean it up with a wire brush so the new tyre would slide on easily. You had to remove the inner tube and gaiter out of the old tyre, check the tube for punctures, remove any rust that was stuck to the gaiter and then fit the tube and gaiter into the new tyre. When you had done all this you put the rim onto a block of wood, coated the tyre and gaiter with soft soap and slipped it all onto the wheel rim. Having done that you refitted the collar and split ring, making sure that the split was opposite the valve, and when this was done you had to put 10lbs of air pressure into the tyre to inflate it and ensure the rim was bedded down by tapping it round. After that was done you could blow the tyre up to the correct pressure. Joe said that if you didn't bed the rim in properly it could fly off and kill somebody and the hardest part would be getting your head down off the Regal roof. (Unfortunately, years later that was how he died).

When the wheel was ready you had to refit it to the lorry. If it was a back wheel there were usually two wheels to fit and you had to put the valves opposite, put the wheel nuts back and then tighten them up with a wheel-brace and a big tube over the wheel-brace for extra tightness so they wouldn't come off. They usually had eight or ten wheel-nuts to tighten up.

One day I was fitting two new tyres on the front of a car and I forgot to let the jack down. As I tried to drive it back I wondered why the steering was so easy to turn and then I realised what I had done – what a wally I felt!

A proper Apprentice

After about two months I went back to the main garage at Vearows Place. The jobs I was given to do when I returned were a lot more interesting. Mr. Breeze let me do engine tune-ups which involved plugs, points, cleaning the carburettor out, and setting the ignition timing. We didn't have any timing lights then so we had to advance the distributor till the engine started to make a tiggling noise which was called 'pinking' and then retard the distributor till the pinking stopped. I also started to decarbonize engines and grind in engine valves. I was allowed to do clutch replacements, relining brakes and other types of general repairs. I learned quite a lot.

I got my first taste of working on commercial vehicles when I had to service a big box van belonging to Cheshire County Council which was used to deliver school meals around the district. It was driven by a man named Walter whom we got know very well. We also did repairs for the ambulance service and when we had finished road testing we used to ring the bell on the front of the ambulance and people got out of the way very quickly!

By this time I was fed up with going out on to the river bank to go to the toilet because there weren't any lavatories in the building. It was not so bad for just a wee but if you wanted to do something else it was rather unhygienic and you also had to watch where you were walking.

While I was working at Breeze's I learned a lot about Solex, Zenith and Stomberge carburettors. Mr Breeze, knew all about them because he was the main agent and sole stockist for these makes. He taught me how to repair them, service them and to change the jets to get the best petrol consumption.

One night when I was going past J.W. Foster and Sons, just down the road from my home at Lostock Gralam, Mr. Fred Foster stopped me and asked me where I was working. When I told him he said that he had a vacancy for an apprentice and if I was interested I could have the job, so the next day I told Mr. Breeze that I wanted to leave. He was disappointed because he said that I was a good worker and could be trusted to do the jobs I was given.

The following. Monday I started at Fosters Garage but I was a bit upset when Fred Foster said that he couldn't pay me as much as I had been getting at Breezes because I had been getting six-pence per hour above the national rate for an apprentice. But I stayed there because it was so close to home and I wasn't that bothered about money anyway. I also liked working there.

Mr Foster said that we could call him 'Fred' when we were on our own but 'Mr Foster' when there were customers about, which was fair enough. After I had been there a few weeks Fred said that he would have my apprenticeship agreement drawn up and that I would have to get Dad to sign over a sixpenny stamp to seal my apprenticeship with them. Fred was the oldest son and in charge of the garage. He was about 40 years old and his younger brother Bill, who was about 35, was in charge of the petrol pumps. Their dad, whom we always addressed as 'Mr Foster' ran the machine shop. The machine shop was very well equipped with lathes, grinding, milling and drilling machines, and was equipped to do all engineering work. He was very well known locally for his engineering skills and had been the top foreman at Rolls-Royce at Crewe Works. Fred had been foreman mechanic there during the war.

It didn't take Fred long to find out how much I knew about the job and how much I had learned at Breezes because I did most jobs by myself. He knew that if I got stuck with a problem that I would go and ask him how to sort it out – which wasn't very often. The hours of work were the same as at Breezes but if you had to work after midnight you could start work at 9am the next day. Another good thing was that there was no 'can lad' and the youngest used to go to the café for the tea and toast at baggin time. The woman who owned the cafe was called Betty. She was a well-fed lady and was very pleasant to us lads when we went round.

Other advantages of my new workplace were that we had a toilet and a sink with hot and cold water, a big stove to keep the garage warm and a table and chairs so we could eat our baggin in comfort. Therefore I didn't mind too much about the lower pay and made it up with overtime.

When I had been there a while and had got into the working

practices I started working from 9am until any time after midnight seven days a week, because I wanted to learn as much as I could about the motor trade – cars, vans, lorries and buses. I used to work about 100-110 hours a week and in that time I did learn a lot. As I have said, I had learned to weld and do basic bodywork at Breezes. I told Fred that Mr. Breeze had also taught me how to drive and ride a motorbike, so he allowed me drive cars in and out of the garage.

Fred let us lads take a 40-gallon drum of petrol to Stubbs Salt Works once a month. We used to take it in turns to deliver the petrol. There were four of us – Nev, Dereck, Arty and myself – and we used a 1937 Ford 8hp van to deliver it to the salt works. We could get there by private roads and that's how we gained a lot of experience at driving. Bill used to come with us and sit in the passenger side because he could drive and keep us out of trouble. Fred would decide who went and usually it was the lad who had done the most work in that month. One day Nev took the petrol to the salt works. He had been bragging about what he could do to the girls who packed the salt so they took his pants down and rubbed salt all over his bum and elsewhere. He was red raw when he came back and Fred said that it served him right for being so cheeky to them. He was very quiet the next time he went!

As I have said I worked a lot of overtime and would turn out on to breakdowns and smashes no matter what time – often after midnight. We had a 1934 27 hp. Bedford breakdown truck with a manual crane on the back so we could lift cars and light vans up to bring them back to the garage for repair. It had a 6 volt electrical system and the battery was usually flat because it wasn't used very much but it had a Magneto and only needed a couple of turns with the starting handle before it would start up. It also had an Autovac (this was before the mechanical petrol pumps were fitted) and a Solex down draft carburettor. It had cable brakes and a crash gearbox – there were no synchronized gears then, they came much later.

About this time I started to feel that life had nothing to offer any more and I became very depressed. When I told Mam she made me go to the doctor who said that I was spending to much time working and that I should take up a hobby, so I decided to go and watch the Denville Players on a Friday night. After a few weeks I began to feel all right again but I carried on going to see them.

We used to put exchange engines into cars and overhaul engines, gearboxes, rear axles, front axles and steering boxes. I liked changing Ford engines best because I could change them in three hours while it took the main agents four hours. I liked all the different jobs we had to do (changing and relining brakes, over-hauling clutches, servicing, changing oil filters and tyres) which I found quite easy.

Fred received a letter about us not attending night school so we had to go twice a week from 6.30-9pm on a Tuesday and Thursday. I stopped going after a year because I told Fred that I learned more at the garage so I didn't go again – but later on I got qualifications in the Army.

One day I was sharpening a chisel on the grindstone and a piece of steel went into my eye because I wasn't wearing goggles. Fred had told us to wear them when we were using the grind-stone but we thought that we knew better. He said that if we would not be told, we had to learn the hard way – which I did! Fred sent me to the doctor, who tried to take out the metal, but he found that it was in too deep and said that I would have to go to Manchester Eye Hospital to get it removed. I remember the pain that I had going to the hospital – I filled two handkerchiefs with tears before I got there. They got it out and I had to wear a patch over my eye for a week, so Fred put me on light duties doing odd jobs.

One day there was a bad smash on the A556 Manchester Road between a motor cycle combination and a car. Fred told me to get the breakdown vehicle ready and to take my time checking the oil and water so that the police and ambulance men would have time to sort things out and get the injured to hospital before we arrived and we wouldn't have to see all the "blood and gunge" as he put it. I filled the breakdown lorry up with petrol, oil and water. The battery was flat as usual so I had to swing the engine by hand. First you had to check that the gear lever was in neutral and turn the engine over without the ignition switch on about six times, then make sure that the advance and retard lever was in the retard position – if it wasn't, and the ignition was switched on, it would kick back. Fred said that to swing the engine you had to have your thumb around the handle so you could hold on if the engine kicked back and it wouldn't swing round and break your wrist. There was a lot of controversy over whether to put your thumb around or the same side as your fingers, but I found that it was best to do as Fred said. Then you pulled the choke out, switched the ignition on and when you turned the engine over it would start up. After the engine had started you put the choke half way in, the advance lever to 'advance' and when the engine was warm it would tick over.

When Fred came we went to bring the car and motorbike in. He was right about taking your time going out to an accident, unless the police told you differently, because when we got there the injured had been taken to hospital. We had to take the car and motorbike to Northwich Police Station so they could be examined for road-worthiness and the cause of the accident could be blamed on the right person for insurance purposes. When we got to the police station I unhitched the car and motorbike from the break-down while Fred was talking to the Police Inspector about the accident. When we were ready to go Fred asked me to start the breakdown ready to go. I switched on the ignition but I had for-gotten to check that it was out of gear and when I turned the engine over it started up. I felt such a fool, but I managed to jump into the cab and pull it out of gear. The police who were watching couldn't stop laughing at my antics. When we got back to the garage, Fred told me off for showing off in front of the police. He warned me to be more careful in the future as I might not be as lucky again and get hurt by being careless.

I was still working a lot of hours but on a Sunday I was doing more gardening than repairs on cars and Fred let me charge for small repairs such as sorting out miss-firing, fuel blockages, water leaks and punctures and told me to keep the money. But being a sucker for a hard luck story I didn't make much money, anyway.

While we were waiting for breakdowns on Saturday afternoons and Sunday, I planted two big lawns around Fred's house and also built a rustic fence for climbing roses. I had to start going to night school again so that I could get my National Service deferred till I was 21 years old. Then I got fed up with going again and carried on working at nights and weekends. One Sunday a man came into the garage with a puncture in the back wheel of his motorbike and said that he was on his way home to Blackpool and didn't have much money. I couldn't see him stuck for 4s 6d which was the price of a puncture repair and so I didn't charge him when I had done it. When I told him I wasn't charging him for the repair he took a parcel out of the pannier bag and gave it to me because he said that he was very grateful. When I opened it was about two pounds of home-cured bacon and when I took it home Mam was very pleased and sliced it up. As I am telling you this my mouth is watering, because I can still taste it after all these years.

Another time Fred told me off was one Sunday when a Hillman broke down with overheating. When it pulled into the garage I lifted the bonnet up and gave my opinion as to what the trouble was, telling the owner that the cylinder head gasket had gone and it wouldn't take us long to do. But when I took the cylinder head off, the gasket looked like a new one and I had ask Fred what was wrong with the car. He told me it was a cracked valve-seat and to test it I would have to fill the engine block up with hot water which I did. After about five minutes the water leaked out of a crack between number 3 and 4 valves on the second cylinder alongside a water port. Fred had let me carry on making a fool of myself in front of the customer to teach me a lesson and to stop me being so clever and big-headed. I found out later that the customer owned a garage in Manchester and was a friend of Fred's.

About this time I did a complete overhaul on a 1939 Standard 14hp saloon. I did everything on it – overhauling the engine, gearbox, putting in a new clutch, steering, steering box, brakes and new brake cables, wheelbearings all round, checking and repairing all the window winders and door catches, repairing and resetting the roadsprings, making and welding patches into the holes in the floor, doors and mudwings, spraying underneath with bitumen to stop the rust and then respraying the whole car black. After all that work Fred and I took it on test and all that I had to do when I got back was to readjust the brakes. Most of the brakes that were used on cars at this time were Bendex cable brakes, which were used on Rootes Group cars, and had to be set up in a special way or they wouldn't work properly.

After I had overhauled that Standard 14 there was no stopping me and I thought that I could do anything because Fred had been very pleased with me. And I must admit my head swelled to twice the size. But it soon went down again when I de-coked a Standard 9 hp. I drained the water out and took it into the garage to work on where I took off the cylinder head and took out all the valves, cleaned all the carbon off all the parts, ground all the valves in and reset the tappet clearances which had to be done to thousandths of an inch or they would rattle and make a noise. When I started the engine up and got it running it sounded lovely and then after a bit it began to misfire and only run on three cylinders. I checked the plugs, points, plugleads and the carburettor but it was to no avail. I had to take the cylinder head off again and I found a piece of wire from the wire brush had got stuck under No 3 Exhaust valve so there was no compression on No 3 cylinder which in turn made the engine misfire. I had to regrind the valve on No 3 in again and put it right. Fred said that it was unlucky but it served me right for being such a know-all bugger. After that I started to engage my brain first instead of my mouth.

Fred had bought Humber Super Snipe for his personal use and we also used it for breakdowns because it was so big that we were able to tow most cars into the garage, if we had to, for repair – but most times we were able to mend them at the roadside. After Fred had had the Humber for about a month it started to run on five cylinders so I was given the job of finding out what the trouble was. I took the cylinder head off and we found that it was badly warped and needed planing, and also that No 12 exhaust valve was cracked. Fred said that I had better de-coke the engine, so I cleaned all off the valves and the block, replaced No 12 valve with a new one, reground all the rest in and reset the tappets ready to refit the cylinder head which Fred had planed. I fitted a new head gasket, put the head back on and tightened all the cylinder head nuts as tight as I could. There weren't any torque spanners then and all you could do was to tighten the head nuts up as tight as possible. I started the engine which ran 'as sweet as a nut' as we said in the motor trade.

After about two months the Humber started to missfire once

more and when I stripped it down No 12 valve was cracked again and Fred said the compression ratio was too high after planing the head. I had to make a special cylinder head gasket so I got some $\frac{1}{8}$th aluminium plate and a head gasket, drew the shape on to the aluminium and made a gasket. I fitted it back on the engine with copper and asbestos gaskets either side of the aluminium gasket, put the head back on, tightened all the nuts up, ran the engine until it was hot and then retightened everything again. It was still running well years later, so I must have cured it.

One of the best things was going out with Mr B. Foster, the 'Big Boss', as we called him, which was a laugh in itself because he was only 4ft 8ins tall. He had a 1939 Standard 8 black two-door saloon and when you opened the door his Alsatian bitch Meg would jump into the car because he took her everywhere. It was good working with the Boss because you did engineering jobs with him and also you had some fun because he had virtually gone back to his second childhood and we used to go conkering and play conkers.

There was an outside toilet and all the men that worked at the salt and rubber works used to call for a wee. It started to smell too much in summer and the Boss decided to wire the toilet up. He got a transformer to drop the electricity voltage down to 100 volts saying that he didn't want to hurt anybody, just give them a fright. It worked and they stopped using it. We had a good laugh when we saw what happened. Another time when Meg was on heat there was always a little mongrel dog hanging about who fancied his chances. The Boss got fed up with chasing him off and told me to catch him and hold on to him. I didn't know what the Boss was going to do but he had gone into the house for some Sloane's Liniment (people my age will know what that did) and rubbed it on to his testicles. He said to let him go so I did, and when it started to work the dog went down the lane like a rocket and stopped to lick himself off and the Boss said that he must have run out of Sloane's. Needless to say the mongrel never came back.

I enjoyed working in the machine shop with the Boss because there was a nice atmosphere and if you did the job that he gave you to do properly he would be happy. If you did anything wrong and didn't tell him, he would chase you out of the shop with a 2lb hammer. If he caught you he would hit you with the hammer shaft, not the head so it wouldn't hurt you, and he would explain afterwards what you had done wrong.

The other son, Bill, was a nice bloke but he'd had a bad accident when he was younger and it had left him a bit slow. However he was basically very intelligent and was in charge of the petrol pumps and tyre repairs, and he also did all the crankshaft regrinding for the engine overhauls. When you filled up Fred's car Bill would always make sure that you only put National Benzine Petrol in the tank. When I asked Fred the reason and he told me that every two months it was 100 Octane and that made the engine run better.

I was first introduced to heavy goods vehicles when I had to go to Brombrough near Chester to tow a Leyland Lynx in that had broken the timing chain. We towed it with a rope and Fred warned me to keep the rope tight by touching the brakes now and again so that I wouldn't get them too hot and cause brake fade. He also said I had to keep the brakes off when we were going uphill and to just touch them when we were going down so that I wouldn't run over the rope. We got back to the garage all right and he gave me the job of putting on a new timing chain and retiming the engine. He was amazed when I did it by myself and I told him that Mr. Breeze had shown me what to do. It ran very well, so after a test run Fred took it back.

Near to the garage was Joseph Parks Steel Works. Mr. Paddy Denton was a director and he had an S Jaguar sports car that he used for rallying and hill climbing at weekends. On a Monday he brought it in to be worked on. We had to put it on the outside ramp to wash off all the mud and dirt with a high pressure hose (150psi) and then take it into the garage for a service and oil change. After we had serviced the car we put it back on the outside ramp and made a mixture of Red X, old engine oil and paraffin and sprayed underneath the car ready for the next time. When Mr. Denton came to pick it up he would give 2s 6d to whoever had done the job.

I still went to see the Denville Players on a Friday night and I started to catch the 10.30pm bus home because one of the actresses, Mary Quinn, and her actor husband Robert Donut caught the same bus. I got to know them quite well and when I told them that I worked at Fosters Garage they said that they lodged at a house at the back of the garage. Years later Mary Quinn got a part in 'Coronation Street' and I felt very proud that I had known her.

About this time I got a septic finger and the doctor put me 'on the club' for a week. I was still working at Fred's home at the weekends while we waited for breakdown call-outs. Fred's wife was in bed with the flu and he said that to save me having time off I could look after her and make his dinner for him. I made them egg and chips every day for a week and Fred said that he would be glad when his wife was better because that he was fed up with bloody chips!

At this time of the year the work in the garage was very slack and there wasn't very much to do so when I went back to work Fred had decided to have a wall built on the top of the showroom so that he could display the garage's name and put up the RAC and AA accreditation signs. The wall was built by Mr. Alf Cooper who was the foreman brick layer for Fred Whitehead & Sons Ltd. I did the labouring. When it was finished and the name was put up, with the illuminated signs on either side, it looked very good.

While we were still slack Fred decided to make a rota for us to work at night because we were not busy in the garage and to be fair we should take it in turns to work from 5pm until 10pm till the work picked up again. We lads would then get about the same in pay.

When I was 18 years old I had to register at the Labour Exchange for National Service, like all the other teenagers at that time, because it was the law. I got deferred till I was 21 years old but I had to go to College one day a week and to Night School three nights a week. The work in the garage was very slack so one Monday night when it was my turn to work I asked Fred if he wanted me to come back that night. He said that since we had been slack all day it was a daft question and, no, he didn't. I decided to go and help out with the harvest at Greenways Farm at Tabley. Phillip told me to get Captain, a big 17hh chestnut Shire horse out of the stable, harness him to a four-wheeled cart, put thripers on to the cart and to bring the corn in out of the top field.

(Thripers were put one at the front of the cart and one at the back so that you could get a lot more corn on the cart). I did and when we had loaded it I took it back to the farm to unload alongside the Dutch barn. You had to throw the corn stooks on to the conveyor belt with a pikele and they would be stacked for winter or when the thrashing machine came. When I went to work the next day Fred called me into his office and played bloody hell with me saying that he had wanted me to work on the Monday night and that I hadn't come back. When I told him that I had asked him if there was any work and he'd said that there wasn't, he didn't remember and said that I should make my mind up whether I wanted to be a mechanic or a farmer. He warned me that if it happened again I would find myself in the Army. I was very upset that after all the work and jobs that I had done around his house, and all the extra work I had done for him at the garage, he could

Me when I joined the Army

just send me into the Army without a second thought. I was over 18 years old now and I thought, "Well, if that's the way he wants it, I'll show him what he can do with his job!"

I decided to go into the Army as soon as possible, so I went up to the Recruiting Office at Castle in my dinner time and got the details about joining up. The Recruiting Sergeant said that he would take me to Chester the next day for a medical examination and if I passed I could join the Army. I passed that with flying colours ('A1' as it was then). But when I went back to the Sergeant and told him that I had passed the medical he said that I couldn't do my National Service because I had been deferred until I was 21 years old. I could only get in if I signed on as a regular soldier for three years minimum and if I did that I would get all the privileges such as 30 days' paid leave and four travel warrants a year. I thought "What's a year in your life when you're young?" and so I signed on for three years with the Colours and four with the Reserves. The Recruiting Sergeant said now that I had signed on as a regular I could take my pick of the Regiments that I wanted to go into – although at 5ft 4ins I wasn't tall enough to go in the Guards – so I decided to go in The Royal Engineers. Then I had to take the Loyal Oath and after I had done that he gave me the Queen's shilling and I was well and truly in the Army. I was told to report to No 1 Training Regiment Royal Engineers at Malvern, Worcestershire, on 29th August 1952 (coincidentally Dad's 42nd birthday). As that was a month away I decided to go and work at Greenways Farm when I'd finished at Fosters.

When I went into work the next day and told Fred what I had done and that I would have to finish on Friday, he said that I couldn't because that I was deferred till I was 21 years old. I said that I had signed on for three years and was now classed as Army personnel. He told me that I could finish a week on Friday, so I worked a week's notice. He gave me a lot of good jobs to try and show me what a fool I had been to be that hasty, but I was still very hurt and didn't care. Anyway it was too late and I had to go in the Army.

When I left Fosters I went to the farm to get fit enough to be a soldier. We picked potatoes in the mornings so that the sun had time to dry the dew off the corn and in the afternoon we got the corn in. I worked with Captain, my favourite horse. We would go into the corn field and when I got off the cart, George, who was an Irishman, got on so that he could stack the corn as I threw it up to him. When I had thrown one stack up I just shouted "Gee up" to Captain and "Whoa" we got to the next stack. When the cart was loaded I took it back to the farm. We milked the cows – pedigree Ayrshires – first thing in the morning and with them being one of the first Tuberculin-Tested herds in the county we had to be very hygienic and wear white smocks, wellingtons and white caps. We had to wash the cows' udders off with disinfectant before we put the milking unit on to each one. When the milk container was full we had to change the milking unit to another container and then take the milk to the dairy and empty it into the cooler. The milk ran over the cooler and through about three sieves into the milk churn. When the churn was full we had to take it to the collection point, which was a platform at the front of the farm. It took two of us to lift the churn on, ready for the milk lorry to collect in the morning.

The end of August came near and most of the harvest was in. There were only the root crops remaining – late potatoes, turnips, mangolds and kale – and then the harvest would be finished for another year. That meant that the day soon arrived when I had to go into the Army.

I had got all the travel warrants for the journey and after saying goodbye to the family – which didn't upset me because I was used to going away to the Scout camps – I caught the train from Northwich to Crewe. I had to wait at Crewe for about half an hour for the train to Worcester. While I was walking up and down the platform I saw a bloke about my age sitting on a seat looking all fed up. I noticed he had a little brown case like mine and so I asked him where he was going. He said "To Malvern to go into the Army" and when I said that I was going to the same place we decided to travel together to keep each other company. We introduced ourselves: he said his name was Ernie and that he came from Wigan where he had been a coal miner. He had been involved in a pit fall, had been very frightened and had decided to join the Army.

Ernie offered me cigarette and was amazed when I said that I didn't smoke and refused to have one. He kept on for me to have one and I thought "What the heck, I'm going in the Army!" so I did. It made me a bit dizzy, but by the time I got on the train I was all right. When we were settled down in our seats Ernie pulled out two bottles of brown ale and offered me one. Again, he was amazed when I said I didn't drink, and he insisted that I had a bottle. I did in the end, and enjoyed it very much.

As we travelled along I thought to myself that on the first day of going into the Army I had started two bad habits and hadn't even got to the Camp yet.

"Well," I thought, "if this is the start of my Army career, I'll have another story to tell..."

THE APPRENTICE FITTER'S TALE:
From Schoolyard to Shipyard

PETER BUCKLEY

This is dedicated to my granddaughter Olivia and any future generations – who were the inspiration to write it in the first place. Also to all my family and friends for their help and encouragement.
PB

Wartime childhood

This is my life story as far as I recall and as accurately as I can remember. I shall try not to use other people's 'memories', but where I have done so shall endeavour to identify that person.

I was born on April 12, 1938 at No 13 Warrington Road, Northwich, which I'm reliably informed was next door to the Ring o' Bells pub. Neither of these fabled establishments is now with us, I'm sad to say. When I was one year old we moved to No 1 Parkfield Road, Northwich.

I suppose my earliest memory is of sitting on my mother's knee one afternoon by the fire, although the sun was shining brightly – so I would guess it was autumn – when my dad came in, and poured hands full of the old twelve-sided threepenny bits into her lap. Each one was so bright and shiny that seemed they must have been collected just for this occasion and I've had a soft spot for that coin ever since!

The story behind this collection of threepenny 'Joeys', as they were known, was, as I learned years later, because Dad was medically unfit for military service, having an enlarged heart, so he, and many others like him, was required to do essential war work whenever and wherever he was needed. On this occasion he was working in Stoke-on -Trent, doing what I have no idea, but apparently he was only able to get home perhaps every weekend or so. The journey then, of course, would take much longer than the 30 minutes it takes the modern motorist, and petrol was rationed which didn't bother Dad as he didn't have a car!

One other memory of this event was of a blue and white sailor suit, which I understand was purchased out of the money so saved. This of course was most probably told to me by one of my brothers or sisters, or even my mother or father.

At this stage, I'd better identify the rest of the family. Dad's name was Samuel, 'Sam' to everyone, and Mother's name was

Barbara and Fluffy the cat

Robert, aged about five years

Merle with Fluffy – she's still potty about cats

Edith Florence (née Boden or Bowden?). My brothers and sisters, starting with the oldest are Alice May, John William, Harry, Lillian, Merle, me, Barbara, and last Robert, who was the surviving twin. As in many families, some of us had nicknames bestowed upon us by Dad. I may sometimes refer to them by that name, so, as I recall them, Alice May was 'Tal', William was 'Bill', Harry became 'Mick', and Robert was 'Barton' – which I think was first my nickname and referred to a radio serial called *Dick Barton, Special Agent*, a sort of latter-day James Bond. Mother's nickname was 'Flip', but I don't know why.

My most vivid memories of the war are of being wakened early in the mornings either by the air raid sirens or by some other member of the family, to be hurriedly dressed and rushing outside past a perfectly good air raid shelter to take shelter next door in Mrs Flatley's house – built exactly as ours was but for some illogical reason deemed to be safer!

A 'memory' I've been told about is of a land mine exploding somewhere over on the "Old Hole", now known as Witton lime beds. I'm told that Tal upended the table, pots and all, pushing it against the window and gathering all of us together behind it to protect us from flying glass. This apparently was standard procedure as laid down by Ministry of Defence.

I can also remember double summer time quite vividly, when it stayed light until eleven o'clock or later, when Kevin Flatley from next door and I ran wild, it seems.

I remember the German prisoners of war in the camp at Marbury. If you explore the woods as I have, you will find traces of their work such as the older wooden plank bridges over the drainage ditches. I think the ditches themselves may have been dug by the prisoners. The great German goalkeeper Bert Trautmann was held here for a while before being moved to a camp at Hyde, I believe, and after the war he played in goal for Manchester City.

Also in these woods are the remains of either an anti-aircraft gun site or a searchlight – at least that is what I understand it to be.

Marbury was later used to house Polish servicemen and refugees, and later still some of the Northwich couples waiting on the housing list. My brother Harry and his wife Dot lived there for a while in the early 1950s, and very cosy it was too.

I should imagine that a lot of Northwich families have mementoes of German craftsmanship from this time. I know, for instance, that there is or was a small wooden bowl, about three inches in diameter by approximately two and a half inches tall, at Tal's that I'm told was hand carved by a P.O.W. at Marbury camp. They also made some very good carpet slippers out of rope. These things must have been sold for a few pence to buy extra little luxuries: literally money for old rope.

Although they were prisoners, they were allowed some freedom because I clearly remember seeing them in their brown P.O.W. uniforms around the Marbury area, if not the town. I suppose like the allied P.O.W.s they were put to work on farms and such like.

In 1943, when I was five years old, I started at Timber Lane School which, for the benefit of those who did not have the pleasure of attending this seat of learning, was situated just about where the newer part of Woolworths, Argos and the precinct square are now.

The only bits I remember from this period are learning to play "catch a girl, kiss a girl", being a virtuoso on the clappers in the music class and colliding violently head to head with Joe

Moores as he came out of the toilets and I went in. The result was two bloody noses and Joe and me becoming good friends during our later school days.

However, I did witness a bit of drama one day, with Merle, and maybe Lillian, on the way home for our dinner (this was before we called it 'lunch'!), when, as we were walking across Station bridge, a U.S.A.F. four-engined bomber, possibly a B17 or a B24, or even a B 29, flew over heading in the direction of Crewe. As we watched, the tail fin slowly fell backwards! We were on top of the bridge and, as I can distinctly remember looking down the railway lines which run parallel to Victoria Road, I must have been held up by someone to be able to have seen it. At this point the plane was probably over the River Dane roughly behind the Danefield estate. Now, at only five years old, I must have known that bits do not fall off aircraft under normal circumstances and so I did the only sensible thing, I ran home as fast as I could screaming at the top of my voice – only to be rewarded with a clout to the side of my head from my dad. I'll give him the benefit of the doubt and say he was only trying to shake me out of my panic, which was quite considerable. I never did find out what became of that bomber.

One benefit of the war, as far as I was concerned, was the wonderful food parcels sent to the people of Great Britain. I had my very first taste of canned peaches from one of these.

Like most people of my generation I recall seeing the red glow in the sky over both Manchester and Liverpool after a raid by German bombers as the cities burned. How lucky we were to be living in such a quiet area and not subjected to the same ordeal.

One day while out in the backyard, doing little but helping my Mam talk to Mrs Southern, a Spitfire or possibly a Hurricane roared over Southerns' house literally a few feet higher than the rooftops, so low we could clearly see the pilot as he waved and waggled his wings. I like to think he waved at me! On reflection, it must have been at the end of the war.

MAP OF SHIPBROOK AREA IN NELLIE OSBORNE'S YOUTH

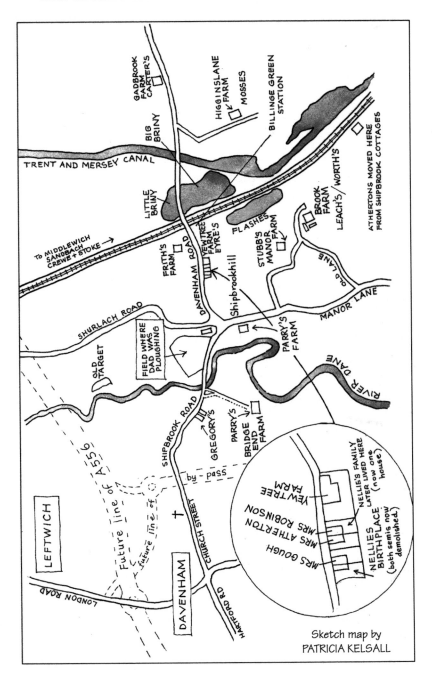

Sketch map by
PATRICIA KELSALL

MAP SHOWING LOSTOCK OF GEOFF MELLOR'S YOUTH

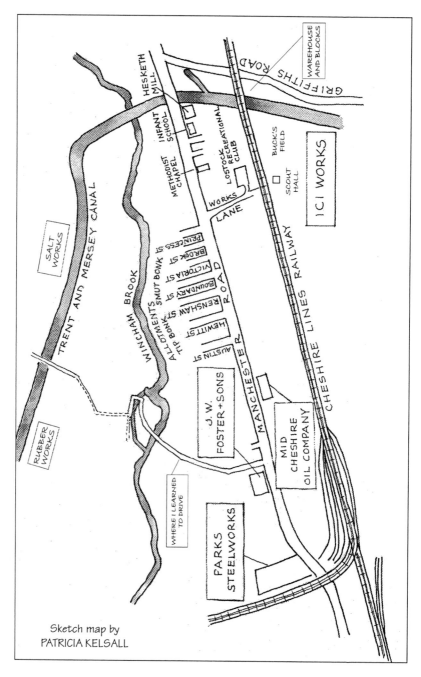

Sketch map by
PATRICIA KELSALL

b

NORTHWICH MAP SHOWING YARWOOD'S AND BREEZE'S

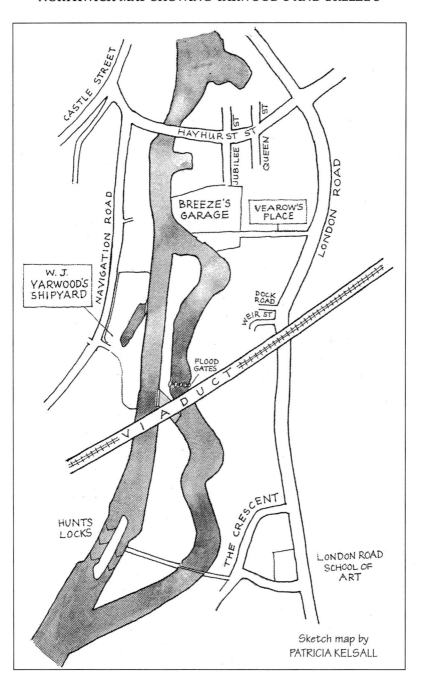

Sketch map by
PATRICIA KELSALL

MAP OF RAILWAYS IN NORTHWICH IN THE DAYS OF STEAM

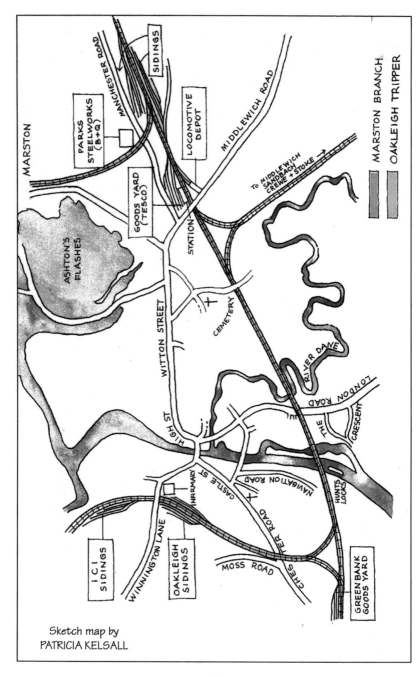

Sketch map by
PATRICIA KELSALL

d

Because the first six years of my childhood were spent during the Second World War, the luxuries we tend to take for granted now were in very short supply then, if they were available at all. For instance, turkey was not – we were probably lucky to have a chicken – and I'm sure many a family did not enjoy even that little luxury. However, we still enjoyed our Christmases, and I have some very fond and amusing memories of them. Also some which are not so fond.

Merle (seated), me and Barbara about 1945-46

On the brighter side a couple of events that made us laugh then, and still bring a smile, are as follows. Electric tree lights of course were things of myth and legends, but we did have clip-on candle holders, and although they were obviously dangerous we were permitted to light them occasionally. On this particular Christmas Day, Merle decided to light ours with a paper spill ignited from the fire, and as the paper burned down and began to lick around her fingers, she dropped it right into the tree. I don't know what the flash point of pine is, but in seconds this one was doing a pretty good imitation of a Yuletide barbecue! The flames were quickly reaching for the paper garlands hanging from the ceiling, when Mother, alerted by the shouts of alarm, rushed in, assessed the situation, rushed out, filled a bowl with water, got half way back and said something like, "Oh dear me, this is HOT water!" then ran back to the kitchen for cold water! Luckily our Harry, always the brainy one, had opened the window and chucked the burning tree out. This, as I say, still makes me smile but it could have been a tragedy, and I may not have had the chance to write this now were it not for Harry's quick thinking.

Another amusing memory was on the occasion when on one Christmas Day, Dad, who had gone out for his Yuletide luncheon pint, came home so late that we had all eaten – not an unusual event in many families, I have to say. On this day he had with him my Aunt Beatie, Uncle Vin and Uncle Johnny, all in their cups, as they say, and it all got rather merry, especially when Uncle Vin helped himself to another cup of tea and poured custard into it instead of milk. Of course, not wishing to appear rude and interrupt his conversation, we all kept quiet and enjoyed the expression on his face as he endeavoured to drink it.

As I've already said, goods were scarce, so many of our toys were second-hand or home-made, and I remember a wonderful bright red locomotive, made by my dad from wood. Another time it was a Wild West fort, complete with lead cowboys and Indians. When he wanted to, he could be quite good with his hands.

The choice of Christmas trees then was very limited, unlike today when there is so much choice it can be confusing. I seem to recall only having a large branch from a pine tree, or an artificial one made from a brush handle with bottle washers dyed green and stuck in to form 'branches'.

The decorations too were usually home-made from coloured paper and anything that our imagination deemed suitable, for instance, someone managed to obtain rolls of silver foil, about an inch wide, and this was made into garlands by repeatedly folding one strip over another to make a sort of chain, or maybe they would be cut and glued into linked loops. It was not until many years later that I was told that this was aluminium foil used by the Royal Air Force bombers to 'dazzle' the German radar – what the R.A.F. called 'chaff'. Just how we got it I do not know, maybe it was at the end of the war and was no longer needed for its primary role.

Other tree decorations were small books bought from Woolworth's for a few coppers. These were only about four or five inches high by two or three inches wide, and they contained condensed versions of all the classic stories such as *Sinbad the Sailor, Aladdin, Treasure Island* and *Snow White*. They would be hung on the Christmas tree and distributed when the tree was taken down on Twelfth Night. My brother Harry could never wait for this, though, and would read them in situ. The only sound from him for a while was the occasional shuffle of his feet as he moved to another one of the books. As these same little books seemed to be a regular tree feature, he must hold the world record for the number of times he had read them!

Although most of the world's people were trying to kill each other, we children were quite safe to run around the streets and countryside at will, without fear of child molesters and murderers. And we certainly did run around, because we had no T.V. and radio for the most part was geared for adults. We had to make our own amusements, which usually consisted of rough street games, especially in the evenings, such as "Kick can", "Deleavo" and "Jack, Jack show your light", to name but a few. For the most part they involved a lot of running, chasing and shouting, the very things which would get me labelled a "hooligan" now (by me as well, I suspect).

Some time around this period, I saw the Northern Lights. I swear to this, even though I've been told we are too far south for me to have done so.

If we were not running about the streets, then we were running about along the fields by the River Dane. A favourite though simple pastime would be jumping the brook which runs into the Dane, which I learned many years later is called Gad Brook, 'Gad' being a corruption of the word 'God'.

There were then certain places on this brook where one could

My mother

jump from one bank to another, some being more difficult than others. At that time, a family named Booth lived over on Danefields. There was Peter, about my age, with whom I later became close friends, and his two older sisters, Thelma and Doris (or maybe Dorothy), and these two always seemed to set both the course and the standards. This must all seem very simple, rustic even, to modern readers, but that was all we had. We kept fit and enjoyed ourselves.

Every pastime then had a "season", for instance in the winter months it was almost always those street games mentioned earlier, and also when it was freezing, we would make slides on pavements and ponds if the ice was thick enough, which it always seemed to be. November of course was the month of Bonfire Night, and we would be guarding the hard-won bonfire wood we had gathered in October – or pinched from some other bonfire, more likely, which was why we were guarding ours! We all vied with each other to make the best Guy, because the best Guy got the most money from passers-by, to our cries of "Penny for the Guy, Mister!" The most favoured spots were outside one of the three cinemas in Northwich, where the courting couples were the most generous, as the lad would be trying to impress his girlfriend. Sometimes we would take the Guy around the houses, when we did a bit of 'soul caking', and for the big night of November the Fifth, we may have gone chestnutting, and perhaps borrowed a few potatoes from some farm field.

December saw us out again carol "singing"(?). One year Merle and some others dressed me up as a girl and we did very well out of it, as I recall!

When spring came around again, someone – as if by a secret command – would make a catapult, or a bow and arrow. The rubber for the catapult was usually a couple of feet of bicycle valve rubber tubing, bought for a few pence from Jack Gee's bicycle shop on the station bridge – one of several shops on the bridge then – or it would be time to go fishing with a garden cane and a cotton line with a worm tied on the end for bait.

My friends and I spent many a happy hour at Doddy's Pit as we knew it. This was a pond on the field of Tommy Dodd's farm, off Middlewich Road. It is now occupied by Hargreaves Road and the new Hyundai car show room.

Here we would fish for Jack-Sharps or 'Jackies' as they were also known then, now of course they would be called minnows or sticklebacks. Here we also tried to catch the elusive askers, it was not until many years had passed that I found out the correct name was newts, or even efts. I have since learned from the dictionary that 'askers' is an old English name for them, so we were right all along.

Very occasionally a real angler would try his luck on this pond but I never saw anything more exciting than the odd bike frame or bucket arise from the depths for their efforts.

In the winter the pit would freeze over and become our skating rink, not that anyone had skates, but if you were lucky enough to wear clogs or even boots, then they were the next best things.

In springtime the woods at Marbury beckoned when the bluebells were in full bloom. In the wood which I now know as The Hop Wood, Marbury brook ran bright and clear. It still does, thank goodness. Over the brook by a little beach was always a rope swing. The really athletic types could and did swing over unto the far bank, which was much higher. I never managed this feat, usually being too afraid to let go when my momentum took me back to the beach. The arc of my swing got shorter as my arms got more tired, and I'd let go just in the centre of the brook. Then it was either go home wet and face the wrath of my parents or dry off by a hastily-lit fire, go home reeking of wood smoke – and face the same!

If we managed to collect a sufficient amount of bluebells, sometimes we could sell a few on the way home and make a bit of pocket money. Now it is illegal to pick wild flowers, I am told.

If the weather was really hot we would swim in Marbury mere, entering the water at the end of the mere which is overlooked by the bird hide now. From here we would swim out to an anchored green punt which made a very nice diving platform. We were of course trespassing in those days, as this was long before it became Marbury Country Park. One could wander the woods all day and not see another soul.

Over the years I was to spend a lot of time in this area, because where Mill Bridge is, once there was a saw mill, hence the name, and that branch of the River Weaver known as Witton Brook, into which Wade Brook runs, was in my childhood used as a dumping site for the old worn-out I.C.I. boats. Here they were scuttled and left to rot – and we kids were attracted to them like dogs to lampposts. I and lots of others spent many happy hours exploring them. This was not without its dangers as the holds were usually under water. I think it was a sad end for these great little river craft.

At other times maybe we would make a cart out of a plank and a set of pram wheels and have races, as we did with the bike wheel 'trundles'. If your wheel had a tyre on it you were the envy of all your mates – until some show-off got a car tyre, that is! I could go on about marbles, tops and whips, and so on, but the above gives a pretty fair idea of how we entertained ourselves then.

Schooldays

I don't think I spent too long at Timber Lane School, because soon I was sent to Victoria Road council school, which I loathed. I despised the way we were 'streamed' into A, B and C groups, and the teacher with her plummy voice forcing us to say 'buck' for 'book', instead of trying to teach us to read the bloody books! Needless to say I was for ever in a C group. I think I learned to read despite the teaching staff, not because of them.

One bit of fun we did have here, though, was in the country dancing class when Louis Jarvis, Brian Simpson, Raymond Burgess, Eric Mainwaring and I discovered that if we came to school in wellies we were not allowed to take part in any dance routines. The shame and mortification! This was tantamount to mental cruelty, we had to stand out of sight behind the piano, where we would pass the time reading our comics, so, when we appeared to be hanging our heads in shame, we would be following the exploits of "Morgan the Mighty" or "Desperate Dan." Revenge is sweet if, as in this case, short, because as the number of boys in wellies grew, the dance partners for the girls shrank. Mrs Armitage noticed this and decreed that henceforth on dance days all boys would wear gym shoes or get their legs slapped!

My 11-Plus Exam was a disaster and that's as much on that subject as I'm going to write, except that I failed it, of course.

But it didn't stop us having fun, for we had our own adventure playgrounds long before the term was coined, and just thinking of them makes me wonder how I lived to tell about it.

At Tower Place, about where the Emperor's Court restaurant is now, by a row of cottages where Aunt Beat lived, was a derelict water tower which we would scale via the very unsafe stairs inside, and then climb into the tank on top – for the life of me I can't think why.

From a nearby tip someone would procure a couple of empty

Merle dressed for Northwich carnival, early 1950s

Barbara dressed for Northwich Carnival. (Picture by Lawrence Sands)

forty-five gallon drums, several railway sleepers would appear as if by magic, and pretty soon a raft worthy of Tom Sawyer would be sailing on the then clear waters of The Old Hole. What the sail was made of I do not remember, but the rope lashing the whole together was not always of best quality and often the raft would break up before reaching the promised land. I suppose many a lad (and not a few girls) got their first swimming lesson from these exploits.

The Old Hole had a rough cinder road running across it to Marston, where on a number of occasions I was sent on someone's bike to deliver lunch (or 'baggin' as it was then called), to Dad and our Bill, both of whom were then working behind The New Inn, now somewhat pretentiously renamed The Salt Barge.

To ride across the Old Hole then was a bit of an adventure in itself as the road was often sinking and was in regular need of repair.

The River Dane was another source of fun. It's hard to believe now but people actually swam in the Dane! I did, too, until the early fifties when poliomyelitis broke out in a big way, and, if memory serves me right, everything from swimming to ice cream was held to blame.

The playing field by Church Walk was also a favourite spot, not only for the children but also for adults on some evenings when dances were held there in the large paddling pool. That was a sight to behold, seeing the pool full of people, many wearing raincoats or overcoats if it was a bit chilly, dancing to records – a fore-runner of the dreaded disco! This was soon after the end of the war and I expect that people grabbed their fun where and when they could.

Eventually we had to start growing up, and while we didn't just stop all the above activities, they were curtailed somewhat when I moved up to secondary school.

On 25 March 1949 my grandfather Buckley died aged 76 years, followed on 10 April the same year by my grandmother. When Granddad died my dad took me to see him laid out, and I was encouraged to touch his cold body, my dad believing that to do so would prevent one from dreaming of him.

My grandfather was a tall, moustached, fierce-looking man, very straight-backed and gruff-sounding. I'm sure he was a kind old man but I for one was always in awe of him. I wish I had known him better.

Grandmother was a small round figure, with her hair pulled back into a bun, and I never saw her dressed in anything but black. She reminded me of Queen Victoria, maybe she was in mourning for her still, but more likely she was in mourning for Uncle Billy who was one of the many who failed to come back from the First World War.

My grandparents lived in the last of a row of

My paternal grandparents, Grandmother and Grandfather Buckley

Granddad Buckley with his horses

terrace houses in Witton Street, next to the Green Dragon public house, where I believe the horses that Granddad drove were stabled. These horses were used to pull carts loaded with cast iron pipes and such like to the I.C.I. Works at Winnington from Bates Foundry. (It's long gone now, but some of the machinery can still be seen at Blist Hill Museum at Ironbridge). I'm sure he must have done other journeys too, and I have a fine photograph of him (see above) with a team of two horses and the cart with a load on, posed for outside Verdin Park.

My grandparents' house fascinated me. To get in one had to climb up three steps at the front and back, which was perhaps evidence of subsidence. It was typically Victorian inside and was packed with every kind of treasure, to my mind at least, including stuffed song birds under glass domes, a lovely pair of rearing bronze horses with a semi-draped male figure holding on to the reins, and a wonderful cast iron nut cracker in the shape of a squirrel. Placing a nut in its front paws and pulling the tail down sharply would bring up the paws and crack the nut on the animal's nose. Copper kettles in ever-decreasing sizes gleamed on the hearth. On the walls were framed words of wisdom, two of which I can quote still:

'Tis better to have loved and lost,
than never to have loved at all.'
and
'Who can separate us from
the love of Christ?'

Not bad for a fifty-year memory is it?

If we had the contents of their house now, we could make an Antiques Road Show special, I'm sure. These houses would be classed as slums today no doubt, but to me they were fascinating. The lavatory was an outside privy, there were sheds and other odd structures to explore, and Aunt Bertha and Uncle Johnny lived a few doors away. It must have made a big impression on me because I only recall going a few times.

Apart from the death of my grandparents, 1949 was a joyful year for me as I left Victoria Road school for the last time.

I soon found myself at Rudheath Modern Secondary School for Boys, now Rudheath High School. This is where my education really began, and I learned how to "learn". I'm sorry if this sounds a bit pretentious but I really believe that the teachers here did not give a damn about the status of your parents, or if you were dressed in hand-me-downs, as many of us were, but were concerned with teaching and, more importantly, teaching us how to find out things for ourselves.

This school was also divided into two streams, 'T' for 'technical', and 'R' for 'rural'. I went into 'rural', not being smart enough for the 'T' class. We did a lot of gardening and visiting farms etc., even though very few of us had any intention of working on a farm, but what did we care? We were out in the open air when others less fortunate than us were stuck in stuffy classrooms. The sports field in those days was surrounded by garden plots on three sides, the fourth side butting onto the girl's sports field. The gardens were tended by the pupils and the produce was sold, making money for the school funds.

I had only been at Rudheath for a month or so, when I had an accident. At home one evening, having little to do, Robert and I began to play silly buggers, chasing each other around the

Robert aged about 14 years

table on which our Tal had wool and socks that she was darning. I must have got over-excited and threw a pair of socks at Robert, whereupon he grabbed the nearest thing to him, which unfortunately for me was a pair of scissors! *Smack* – right in my left eye. Luckily for me it was the bit you put your fingers through that hit me and not the point, painful though it was. For some reason I was not taken to a doctor until the following evening, from whence I was whisked to Chester Royal hospital for an emergency operation. I did not know it at the time but my parents were told that I would lose my eye, however thanks to the skill of the surgeon, I still have that eye. It's in a box with my cuff links!!! No, I jest, it's still where it ought to be but my vision is blurred. (In spite of that, I passed my army medical 'A1' – so much for army medicals!)

Robert, if you ever get to read this, I don't blame you, it was all my fault for getting too excited.

When I was told I would have to have my eye out and a new glass one fitted, I was at first very excited. I knew for a fact that no one at school had one, and I was sure when they all saw mine they would be so envious! Of course I did not realise then that a glass eye was only for cosmetic purposes and I would not be able to see with it, so for a while I was a bit disappointed when the doctors said I could keep my own eye.

Almost the next three weeks were spent in the men's ward, where I was spoiled rotten, by both the nurses and the other patients. It was just long enough to save me from being thrown into the holly bush at Rudheath school, which was the fate of all "new" boys.

Then it was back to school, which I have to admit was a bit of a slog. Having missed only three weeks may not seem much, but I always seemed to be hurrying to catch up, and I did.

Slowly I began to get interested in many of the extracurricular activities, such as the school rabbits, poultry, greenhouses and, especially fascinating to me, bee-keeping.

Me in 1953, aged 15,

I was a dismal failure at woodwork, having missed the basic joints stage, but the teacher's perseverance paid off, and I was able to proudly take home a teapot stand, then a lamp and a stool, which were later to adorn the dustbin, as none have survived to the present day – such was the esteem in which my woodworking prowess was held.

Maths were, and still are a mystery to me. English, on the other hand, was my favourite subject, closely followed by History and Geography, in which subjects I was able to pick up sufficient exam marks to keep me off the bottom of the class.

In our third year, we were introduced to metal working, which I loved, and determined not to miss any lessons, I went to the extent of joining the model engineering club after school hours. We were building a steam locomotive. One of my first tasks was to machine and make ready the chimney, which I would insist on calling a 'funnel', much to the annoyance of the teacher, Graham Meridith.

The art class was also a big attraction to me. In the final year we were allowed a free choice period to finish Friday afternoons and, not able to join the metalwork class because it was in great demand, I chose the art class.

All told, I would say I enjoyed my stay at Rudheath and

From left to right: top row: David Piggott, Brian Greatbank, Maurice Riley, Alf Marlow (?), John Palfreyman, Arthur Dalton, Tim Shallcross;
second row: Raymond Heywood, Eric Mainwaring, Maurice Pye, Alan Tickely, Jeff Bland, Colin Johnson, Peter Holland, Peter Buckey (me), Ray Burgess, Teacher, Sammy Dunn;
third row: Harry (?) Harrop, Brian Simpson, Robin Adamson, Neville Prince, Ken Mather, ????, Louis Jarvis, ? Wilson?, Roy Hugh;
front row: Joe Moore (Dewsbury), Peter Yould, Maurice Birkenhead, Keith Wilding, Ken Astles, Douglas Gibbons, Colin Rowe, Fred Whitlow.

those last four years of my formal education, because I stayed on until end of the full year although I could have left at Easter. As most of my friends were leaving then, we had a bit of fun with our teacher Jack Little's cane, which he kept in the stock room at the back of his classroom. He had foolishly given me and two or three others the job of tidying it up, and because it was the last day of term we decided to practise using the long-handled pruning shears on his cane! We left it tied in a neat little bundle on the shelf. At the start of next term, the dozen or so of us who were left were greeted with Jack swishing a nice new cane.

I believe I learned more from Jack Little, Sammy Dunn, Mr Fletcher and Mr Bridges in those two years then I did in the previous six under various other teachers, and I was genuinely saddened to hear of Jack's death in a motor accident, many years later.

During the last two years at Rudheath I began to get consistently high marks in exams – in fact all my exam marks shot up dramatically and I left school being second in my class. All right, I know second out of twelve is not brilliant, but I was not thirteenth!

Let me now say a little about the way our school life was organised. For instance, before entering class, be it morning, noon or playtime, we had to form up into two ranks by class, and were marched in silence into our classroom. If our teacher was not there we would have to wait in silence until he arrived. On one occasion, as we stood waiting our turn to go in, there could be heard a loud metallic clunk, and in front of me a real hand grenade slowly rolled to the feet of Mr Denis Whiteside, who disdainfully asked: "Who dropped that?" When the culprit had sheepishly shuffled forward, Denis just held out his hand, saying: "Hand it over, and collect it from my room at four o'clock." The daft thing was, no one asked if it was "alive" or not!

Another amusing incident which happened in "lines" was that on a number of occasions the Flatleys' dog Rex followed me to school, and would sit down at my heels as if trained to do so. I was ordered to take him home, but he did it so often the teachers must have had their suspicions, thinking that I had trained him to do this, which I had not.

I have mentioned the fruit orchard, but not the fruit, or a fruit in particular, in this case an apple – not just any apple though, this was a prize winner, big, it was THE APPLE! Perfectly formed, beautifully coloured, brilliant red blending into green, but most of all it was BIG! The biggest apple in all Appledom! It was decided to invite the local press to report it, and so the day arrived, and we peasants were put to hoeing the weeds in the orchard, just to give a bit of background colour, so to speak.

Around the corner came the little party of teachers, press, photographers, and some minor dignitaries, and we were all called to gather round and witness the photographing of the biggest apple core in all Cheshire! It had been eaten in its prime on the tree! We never found out who did the dirty deed, but I have my suspicions. I have to say I was very sorry for Old Mr Smith, the headmaster, Jack, Sammy, and the others.

All the teachers seemed to be great characters then. Mr Little could bowl a wicked leg-break and off-break, under-arm! And, although he was partially deaf and wore a hearing aid, he could tell if any one was talking behind him when he was writing on the blackboard. Using his spectacles as mirrors to pinpoint the guilty party, he would suddenly spin around and throw a piece of chalk with unerring accuracy and hit his target each time.

Each and every morning, we had assembly, for prayers, to hear the morning service on the Home Service (now Radio Four). These were conducted by the Head, 'Pop' Smith, later Mr Lewis, and no exclusions. The assemblies could be a bit of an ordeal as we had to sit on the floor to listen to David Kossoff telling his Bible stories, and standing for prayers or hymns was a great relief, believe me! Then on Fridays we would have to sit through the morning concert too! It always seemed to be, Handel (either *The Water Music* or *The Fireworks Suite*), or *The Messiah*, and that's a lot of time on one's pin bones! At the time I hated this music, but I have since come to love it, so Old Mr Fletcher's enthusiasm must have

My sister Alice May ("Tal") in the 1950s

rubbed off. And this teacher was still teaching music and English when Miles our oldest son went to Rudheath, so he could not have been so old.

In our final year at Rudheath, and for our final project to last "the duration", Mr Little decided we should plan our own gardens at home – if you were lucky enough to have one, if not, you had to use your imagination.

This involved drawing up a scale ground plan of our own home complete with house, out-houses and sheds, showing north so that he could advise us on the suitability of the plants we planned to use.

It was then up to us to find out for ourselves what flowers and or vegetables to grow and where. This involved visits to local garden suppliers (there were no garden centres then), to beg for seed catalogues for the information we sought.

All this work was held in ring binders supplied by the school and was lovingly illustrated by us, either with pictures cut out of the seed catalogues or by our own limited artistic skills in drawing and colouring.

For the text Mr Little taught us what I came to believe was his own type of calligraphy, which involved long slender lettering – all the horizontal bars had to line up with each other, as in As and Es for instance. Even my own limited skills at this produced quite an elegant piece of script, I am pleased to say.

Sadly this, along with all my other schoolwork, was soon consigned to the rubbish bin.

Education, like sex, is wasted on the young.

Scrap iron, soft soap and Sloane's liniment

Like all good things, school days had to come to an end, and we pupils were interviewed by the Careers Officer. If ever a person was wrongly titled, he certainly was – "I.C.I. recruiting officer" would have been a more apt name for him, as that was all he had to offer when I suggested I would like an apprenticeship as a fitter/turner at W. J. Yarwood, the shipbuilders. He laughed and said: "No chance, they are not taking anyone on." But he could get me a nice job at I.C.I. brushing up.

That Saturday morning, I, Keith Wilding, and one other whose name I cannot remember, went to Yarwoods, knocked on the office door and asked for a job. All three of us got the apprenticeships we had asked for!

One beautiful August morning I joined my friend John Stanley, who was already an apprentice at Yarwoods, and Sid Moores, and went to work for the first time – walking, of course. That walk alone nearly killed me: Sid must have done his army service in the Gurkha Regiment, as he set such a cracking pace! I was completely knackered when we arrived at The Dock, wearing a pair of grey flannels, a sports jacket and even a tie, as I had been led to believe by John (some friend!) that ALL apprentices started in the drawing office. Only I was sent into the machine shop with Keith Wilding, he looking very smart in his brand-new boiler suit, me looking forlorn in my very unsuitable clothes. I don't remember a great deal about that first day, other than that we were constantly poked and pinched to see if we were real.

The following day I had been equipped with an old faded bib and brace overall and a pair of boots heavy enough to hold a deep sea diver down.

I remember that the foremen invariably wore brownish coloured dust coats over their waistcoats and ties, with a top

Left to right, back row: John Stanley, John Higgins, Peter Buckley (me), Sid Moores; front row: ????, Derek Low, ????

pocket full of pens and pencils, also a requisition book with which to issue orders for goods from the stores.

Whereas many of senior tradesmen and some of the older apprentices always came to work wearing a tie, immaculately ironed shirts and overalls that were well pressed, one man in particular had really sharp creases in the trouser-legs of his bib and brace overalls, and as they never seemed to get dirty I'm sure he changed them daily! These people had bags of style.

Then again there would be those who wore overalls that had so much oil on them that they shone and probably left more muck behind than they kept off the wearers. For some part of my time I was one of those, I regret to say!

In time I adjusted and became just another one of the lads, and was lucky, in that being a little bit older than Keith, he had to make the tea for every one else, while I only had to brew for myself and Ray Lamb, an older apprentice. More about him later.

As apprentices, we naturally came in for our fair share of practical jokes, and we in turn took our revenge in such a manner as to preserve life – ours! For instance, one of us boys had to fill a bucket from the coal-heated water tub, which was also where we brewed tea. This bucket of water was for washing our hands and had to be collected before lunch and before clocking-off time, but often we would forget and it was then a mad dash to get it. On one such mad dash Keith was almost lifted off his feet as he grabbed the bucket in full flight, only to find out the hard way, that some evil bugger had filled it with lumps of scrap metal to just below the level of the water. I think the culprit left half of his coat on the wooden wall where he had hung it that morning, and had snatched at it as he ran for the clocks at clocking-off time – only to discover that it was nailed to the wall. We can only guess 'who done it'.

Coat pockets filled with scrap iron or soft soap, and brew cans nailed to the wooden floors, were fairly regular occurrences. I once found my nice new shiny one-foot rule nailed to the wooden covers of a big face plate lathe and it took me an age to free it.

An old radial arm driller named 'Old Tom' Podmore used to have a sixpenny piece with a tin tack soldered on one side, which he would stick into the floor then wait for some unsuspecting idiot to try to pick it up, when he'd boot them up the backside. 'Yours truly' had to apologise to him because I kicked it first and broke the pin off, so he went to the foreman and complained I'd spoiled his joke! His son, 'Young Tom' Podmore operated a big horizontal boring machine – he seemed old to me then so you can imagine how ancient his dad appeared – but he was really a nice old boy with white hair who was always ready with a spot of advice should you be in difficulty.

As in many factories we apprentices had to endure an initiation ceremony, usually consisting of having one's 'family jewels' daubed with grease mixed with red lead paint or some

At his lathe, Maurice Lockett from Barnton, with whom I had the good fortune to spend part of my apprenticeship. The picture gives some idea of the belt-driven machinery.

such concoction. In my case and also that of Terry Mears, who I think moved from the I.C.I. Avenue works to learn his craft at W.J.Y.s, we were anointed with Sloane's rubbing liniment! The older apprentice, who suggested and provided the stuff, was Derek Wooley, who sadly died recently of cancer, but we bore him no grudges. I had my revenge on him a few days later when I revealed that I had washed off the Sloane's liniment in the mechanical spud peeler used by the canteen cooks which was housed in the same room as the water boiler for tea making!

Before you get the impression we did no work at all, let me tell you we started work at 7.30am during the summer months, and finished at 5.30pm. In the winter we started later and finished earlier but had to work Saturday mornings; this made a 48-hour week, later reduced to 45 hours.

We were normally put to work with an older apprentice or, if you were lucky, a tradesman. I started with Ray Lamb, the apprentice whom I've mentioned before. Ray was one of those men who could look handsome in anything, including dirty greasy overalls, and had no trouble at all in attracting the girls, but he could be a bit moody and switched from being generous to a cruel practical joker. For instance, one day he put me to cleaning out the storage space under the horizontal boring mill we were using to machine iron castings. As I was crouched down he caught some of the iron turnings in a tin lid, and poured them down my neck! Did I jump and swear a bit, I might say. On other occasions as we stood quietly watching the machine do its work, he would reach out and pick up a long spanner and swing it with some force into my hip or rib – he wasn't fussy. Then again he could be so charming and helpful you would think butter wouldn't melt in his mouth.

Soon I was entrusted with a lathe of my own, a Ward collett lathe, bought in with the aid of government money during the war, or so I was told. Here I started screwing rivets, which were used as cheap bolts by the platers to pull the big steel plates together to form the ship's hull.

I think I should just clarify a term here, since then "screwing" has come to mean something quite different. All I was doing was cutting a thread on them. I just thought I'd make that clear before I'm accused of 'rivet abuse'! These rivets were required in their hundreds, as were ladder spills, black steel bars five-eighths in diameter, or the same size square, each end of which was turned down to a diameter of half inch by five-eighths, and were used as the name suggests to make ladders for the ships and the gratings which the crew walked on. These spills were cold riveted between two 2in x ½in flat bars of suitable lengths and were extremely strong. As we had to get many long lengths of the steel chopped in the boilermakers' shop, on the huge power presses, it gave us time and opportunity to see more of the yard and meet people we maybe would not normally meet.

Because I was on this particular lathe, which was perfect for turning pokers, I quickly became very popular with men I'd never met before, and managed to make a few bob on the side. I was busy doing this one day for someone, in between the foreman Harry Dudley's absences from his office, when the crafty old bugger crept up behind me and said: " When you've finished that one, make one for me." So he wasn't such a bad boss after all.

Slowly my apprentice training began to take shape, not in an orderly fashion as one would expect today, more like a teach-yourself course really. For example Harry Dudley would give you a job to do such as, "See Gerald Platt, he wants the hold-ing down bolts turning for engine number so and so" and off you would go have a chat with Gerald, who most likely would send you to Charlie Owen, who was in charge of engineering blueprints (they really were blue then), who would give you the necessary drawings. I would then draw the correct materi-al, steel in this case, and get on with it, visited occasionally by Gerald to make sure I was doing all right and to caution me "not to forget the fillets", a small radius under the bolt head. Once these were turned they had to be fitted, which involved reaming through both the engine base and the engine bed on which it rested, for each and every one had to fit just right and this sometimes meant several trips back and to, so as to get the diameter correct. Any burrs or other sharp edges brought a swift lecture from Mr Platt, and so you learned, and gradually gained experience to tackle bigger, more complicated, and so more costly projects. To spoil an iron casting was bad enough – we had our own foundry, so only a week was lost to cast a replacement – but even more care was taken with a brass cast-ing, which was more expensive both in materials and to pro-duce.

Apart from turning, we were required to use many if not all the other machines. These were millers, borers, planers, shapers and slotters – this last one was a constant source of pain to me. These machines were used to cut key slots in the bore of a pulley, say, which would hold the drive shaft firm, and it involved a bar holding the cutting tool operating in a vertical up and down movement. When slotting cast iron, the swarf built up just on the edge you wanted to see where the guide marking lines were, so naturally one's instinct was to blow it away, but this resulted in iron dust in the eyes and if it wasn't washed out immediately you got a dose of conjunctivitis several days later.

When I started at W.J.Y. most of the machinery was belt driven, that is to say that just one motor drove many machines through a series of shafts, this meant the 'on' and 'off' handles were situated above one's head, so you pulled one down for 'on' and pulled the other for 'off'. All this did was to push the belt from an idling pulley to the driver, and away you went. Sometimes the belt would break, or to be more accurate, the metal fastener would, and this of course would have to be repaired, which we did ourselves – was there no end to our talents? And from time to time the belts would slip, so one of us would throw in a handful of resin to make it grip. Later, when Jack Rowe became foreman, he had all the machines fitted with independent motors. Looking back on those machines now, I realise they were deadly dangerous. 'Guards' were very tall men in bearskin helmets standing outside Buckingham Palace as far as we were concerned! And yet we did not have many serious accidents, although there were some nasty cuts and the odd crushed finger. I had more finger nails torn out than I care to remember, and once had all the fingers and thumb of my left hand skinned, having been taken around a 'vee' pulley. But there were no really bad injuries, perhaps we were more careful because we knew the machines were unsafe. In retrospect, this was probably normal for that period.

On pay-day, everyone would wait outside the pay office, after clocking off, of course, and await their turn to be paid, and it was done in strict numerical order. Naturally, apprentices were amongst the last to be paid. On one such pay day I was being obstructed by someone and made the mistake of swearing at him. Mr Fred Pickford, who was handing the wages out as though it were his own money, which, as he was responsible for it, it was in a way, stopped in the act of handing me my hard-earned pittance and said: "You want your mouth washing out; get to the back of the queue." And I had to do as I was told. It would not happen today, which is a pity, maybe.

The next big treat after that was a launching. These were not only very exciting to watch, and a source of pride, but fun in other ways also, such as the time when a group of students from the London Road College of Art nicely positioned themselves, tutors too, all with sketch pads, directly opposite the tug! Now, a tug may not look very big in the water, low down, but it is very heavy, and when it is launched sideways from the top of the slipway, it is getting a bit of a move on when it hits the water. As these poor buggers found out when several hundred tons of River Weaver hit them! Now you might think

This page and the next: My first launching, the coaster, the Athelbrae, about 1955. To the the right is the 'Dock Hole'. In the top picture overleaf you can see some of the men watching from the bank.

Launch of the Athelbrae

some kind soul would have warned them, indeed one apprentice did start to yell a warning, but had second thoughts when one George Robinson, an ex-Royal Marine Commando, politely requested Alf to be quiet or he would personally throw him in the river, as we stood on the deck of another tug on the stocks. Alf decided to keep quiet.

Further education at W.J.Y. was, on the whole left to the individual, unlike places such as

I.C.I. and many larger and more enlightened employers. I can only remember one apprentice getting day release to attend college and that after hard bargaining by all concerned, such as the foreman and union representatives.

Because all young men normally got called for National Service at 18 years old we were required to attend night school to qualify for the necessary deferment until 21 (22 in some cases) which we did a mixture of enthusiasm and some reluctance.

Mr Alf Turton was storeman, St John's amubulanceman, first-aider, raconteur and practical joker, not to mention social events organiser. On first meeting him although he was not a tall man, he could appear quite stern and a bit fierce, and it took me a while to tell the difference between 'Mr Turton', the serious, and 'Alf', the joker.

One of his favourite practical jokes was played whenever any unsuspecting lad came to him in his capacity as first aid man. If they had a cut finger, a too-regular occurrence, he would become very serious and issue dire warnings about the dangers of losing one's digits if the patient did not pay heed to his medical advice. Then after treating the wound he would open his cupboard and produce a small cardboard box which when opened revealed a finger nestling in cotton wool, complete with dried blood stains – explaining that "this is old 'so-and So's finger", then naming a worker whom you knew to be digitally deficient. This was of course his own finger pushed through a hole in the bottom of the box, but it had the desired shock affect on the victim, for as well as being a very good joke it was also a little lesson in medical after-care. Alf was a wizard with a camel hair brush in removing foreign objects from eyes, and I for one would rather he treated me for this than some of the heavy-handed doctors.

On one occasion he treated a friend of mine for just such a complaint – a bit of metal in his eye. After removing the object Alf distracted my friend by giving him an eye bath to use and telling one of his numerous jokes, finishing by wiping the eye

The Sand Swallow II during a refit - maybe when she was converted from steam to diesel. (Picture taken about 1964 when I'd returned to Yarwood's after doing my National Service).

wash off his face with a wad of cotton wool. T***** was at loss to understand the grins of his work mates as he of course was not aware of profuse white whiskers he had 'grown' due to the cotton wool sticking to several days growth of his own beard and giving him a Father Christmas appearance! *(I have withheld the name to save his embarrassment.)*

Alf ran the works football sweep and sweeps for the big horse races. As most of the men on the yard took part, the prize money was quite considerable and a great financial help to anyone.

Alf also organised regular coach trips to places like Hanley which had a theatre that put on very good shows and brought in stars such as the late Sir Harry Secombe, Ken Dodd, David Whitfield, and many others I have forgotten. He took us on outings to North Wales arranging everything including lunches and the best watering-holes which often ended in a sing-song.

Old Albert Yarwood must have been a bit of a rogue if the stories I was told were true. For instance, on one occasion he went out and bought a centre lathe, the make of which I no longer remember, and on having it delivered to The Dock, promptly had it stripped down to its component parts. Each one was copied in the foundry, machined in the machine shop, and very soon he had three new lathes built by his fitters! All for a fraction of the cost of one new one. I do not know what year this took place, but I did use those lathes, and so far as I know, they were still in use when the yard finally closed down in the late 1960s.

On another of his trips, he spotted an unusual type of lathe in a scrap yard, bought it there and then (he certainly did not let the grass grow under his feet!), and back at Northwich he sent a lorry and driver to collect it. That also was still in use when W.J.Y. closed.

This was a very unusual lathe as I've already said, in that the head and tail stock height could be raised or lowered to suit the size of the work piece being machined. If this is all Double Dutch to you, you will have to get a turner to explain it to you, however, this machine was to cause me a great deal of pain. When I was coming to the end of my 'time' as an apprentice, I was working on this machine when it became obvious that the passage of time had not been kind to it, and especially not to the gear box, which sounded decidedly rough. To me was given the task of stripping said gear box, and "pegging" the broken teeth, which involved removing each gear, filing away the broken tooth or teeth, drilling and tapping a line of holes where the tooth had been, screwing in a piece of stud iron tightly, and then filing these to the shape of the absent tooth. This I duly did and then reassembled the gear box, which now sounded, well, still decidedly rough, to be honest. Just then Jack Rowe, my foreman, arrived on the scene and decided he would like to see the gears in motion.

"Take off the gear box cover," said he, so I did.

"Put it into gear and we'll run it, you hold it in by the gear change handle," said he.

As the gears would not quite mesh I took hold of the 'vee' belts to move the shafts so as to get into gear, at the same time Jack pressed the start button, which swiftly turned the shaft for me, and in the same movement, took my hand once around the 'vee' pulley! Flesh and iron in those proportions do not mix, take my word for it, the result was all my fingers and the thumb of my left hand had the skin and flesh peeled back to the bone, and Jack virtually carried me to the ambulance room, where Alf Turton gently (he assured me) replaced my digital epidermis and sent me to the hospital, where the doctor told me they could do no better than Alf's superb job. With that I had two weeks off work and not a penny in compensation. Oh yes, I almost forgot, apart from an adjustable head stock, and mangling fingers, this machine could be converted into a horizontal borer, which is what I must be sounding like now.

Well, I was getting ahead of myself a bit there, let me tell you how I and everyone else learned to screw cut, also it will give you an idea of the antiquity of some of the machinery.

The first lathe on which I attempted this operation was manufactured by Messrs Reed Inc, of Cincinnati USA, in 1905!

After some rudimentary tuition on setting up the gear trains, etc., I was required to produce a number of Delta metal (a type of brass) spindles, approximately 16in long by seven-eighths diameter, to be screwed two start square thread, left and right hand thread, that is to say, right hand thread for half way, left hand thread the other way. Now I always found thread cutting to be quite absorbing: cutting square threads needed all one's concentration, especially as when you were almost at the end of the cut and needed to wind out the cutting tool nice and evenly, some kindly soul banged a spanner or some such tool on the lathe guard! Needless to say quite a few of these spindles were spoiled due to the tool "digging in" at the crucial moment, causing said spindle to vacate its position from between the centres and describe a disgraceful arc over my head (if I was lucky.) But the job got done in the end.

The launch of another tug at W.J. Yarwood's

Needless to say, this was not the type of machine whereby one pulled a handle here and pressed a button there to set up this operation, but to describe the setting before doing any screw cutting would tax my descriptive powers beyond the limit, suffice it to say that when I graduated to a "proper" lathe the task became much easier.

As I have said before, at Yarwoods as in many factories then if not now, a lot of practical jokes were played, I suppose as a way of letting off steam. We all enjoyed them, unless you were the recipient of course, in which case you just had to grin and bear it.

A regular favourite involved the lavatories which were situated outside facing the dock hole, these were a total of six wooden structures (to serve about 300-350 men) the doors ending about a foot above the ground, having a simple thumb lift catch and "c" handle, and if you were lucky a bolt on the inside. As you can no doubt imagine, these were freezing cold in winter, indeed, they were frozen solid from the first frost,

The Liverpool tug Beechgarth, in 1964.
Note the Northwich gas-holder in the background.

The Beechgarth being towed by her sister ship the Cherrygarth past the Sand Swallow on her way to sea trials. Note the steam train crossing the bridge in the background.

when the water was turned off to prevent bursts. You had to be pretty desperate to use them, nevertheless some did, especially the old hands who went in for a smoke and to make out their bets, or simply to while away the time whilst waiting for the knocking-off whistle. This was the time when the jokers would strike! They would thread a length of one inch pipe through each of the door handles and wait for the knocking-off buzzer. Normally, these doors would then open like greyhound traps, but not on these occasions though: this trick worked particularly well on pay days, when the occupants would only be released when every one else had been paid.

I was told that before I started work there, the toilets did not have individual pans but a common trough running the full length with a stream of water flowing through, much like the Romans used in their military latrines. When this system was in use, the sadistic jokers would try to occupy the upstream trap and, having relieved themselves, would then drop in a wad of burning oily cotton waste, which, as it floated downstream raised the temperatures and the sitters. This was told to me by an older worker and may be apocryphal, but it still makes a good tale.

One of my favourite tricks involved myself, Chris Palin and several others, including Jack Ward, and happened when I had gone back after my National Service, some time in the 1960s. As usual several of us would gather around a stove to share a brew can and eat a butty or two. Every day without exception, Jack would take out two hard-boiled eggs from his bag and, every day, he would tap them on his forehead to crack the shells. Chris and I decided enough was too much, and I took a nice fresh raw egg to work one day! Being a regular kind of chap, Jack would trot off to the bog at the same time each day before his break, and this was when we – well, I – swapped one hard-boiled egg for one raw one. As luck would have it on this day, Chris was on a rush job, and so was unable to join us, but was standing some 60 feet or so away, in time to see Jack crack the first egg, not on his head, but on the stove, and get a sleeve full of embryonic chuckie! Looking up in time to see Chris doubled up with laughter, Jack flew in a rage and threw the other egg at Chris, who fielded it nicely one-handed, tapped it on a nearby stanchion, shelled it, and producing a salt cellar from his pocket, proceeded to eat the aforementioned egg. Jack did not have eggs for baggin there again as far as I know.

Don't think we did nothing but play. At Yarwoods, at least in those days, the apprentices outnumbered the journeymen by about five or six to one, so it is not boasting to say that most of the work was done by apprentices whose ages ranged from 15 to 21 years of age. They would then either be called for National Service, or would join the Merchant Navy to avoid call-up, even though it meant serving five years as against two for National Service, but at least in the Merchant Navy the pay was many times what we received, with the added advantage of continuing one's trade. Even if someone failed the National Service medical they were still made "redundant" so as to force them out into the big cruel world and continue to learn their craft. Hopefully, after a short absence, W.J.Y. usually found a job for you if you asked.

It's a cliché I know, but these were hard times, or at least we thought so. The hours were long, the pay was very poor and the conditions were appalling. For instance the fitting shop and the machine shop were situated under one roof, a leaky roof to be sure, but a roof nonetheless which was more than some of the yard workers had. W.J.Y.'s situation by the river made for some interesting working conditions. Indeed, many a morning we would come into the shop and find a low bank of fog, or river mist, several feet deep, with nothing to see but the odd bit of machinery poking out.

If there had been a frost as well then the cutting fluid on all the machine troughs would be frozen, leaving us nothing to do but to light up the pot-bellied stoves and heat lumps of scrap metal to melt the ice. Even after doing this, the machinery was so cold that as the lathe saddle was traversed it would push a small heap of ice before it as the cutting compound froze when it hit the cold metal slides. It doesn't take much imagination to realise the condition of our hands. If we were lucky to be running a bigger machine then we could take a warm by a stove and also watch the machine (so long as none of the bosses was about). The trouble with this was by warming the rear of our bodies the cold seemed worse on the front, and vice versa!

By lunchtime we were usually thawed out enough to enjoy a game of darts, or just to sit sround one of the stoves and read the *Daily Mirror* to see if Jane was undressing this week! Or we just gossiped. If the weather was good enough some of us would take a walk along the river as far as the little wooden footbridge by Northwich Rowing Club, just to get some fresh air – and to see if any of the Art School girls were about, of course.

Social life

One of the first things I did socially after starting work, was to be persuaded by Keith Wilding to take dancing lessons at Kitty Oakes dance school, then situated in a room over what is now Ian Houghton's camera shop. We learned to do the waltz, quickstep, slow fox trot, rumba, samba etc., and being what I can only describe as painfully shy, this was a difficult time for me, but I survived.

We were taught by Len Breeze, assisted by Glenda McCormack, whom most of the boys, it has to be said, fantasised about. I can still do all those dances but it's the same steps for all, I'm afraid. Anyhow, the sole purpose of the exercise was to gain closer proximity to the opposite and fair sex, but red-heads, and brunettes were quite acceptable.

After a day behind a machine, I and all my friends needed to relax, and as we were in a permanent impecunious state, most

Me at Northwich Regatta, aged 19

of our money was saved for the weekend, mainly Saturday night – the Saturday night dance be to exact. These were arranged in rough rotation at a number of venues, such as I.C.I.'s Lostock Social Club, Winnington Concert Hall (again an I.C.I. Club), The Drill Hall in Darwin Street, the Territorial Army Drill Hall, and even the Baths Hall, in Victoria Road, where the full pool was boarded over for the purpose. Out of Northwich, the Strand Ballroom at Winsford was a regular favourite; this was a converted cinema and boasted its own regular 14-piece band, The

Carlton Players. Upstairs it had a very nice little lounge and coffee bar to relax in.

Because the dances were so popular, it was necessary to buy a ticket weeks in advance for many of them, especially if it was a special occasion such as Christmas Eve or New Year's Eve.

The local bands for these events were Tommy Nichols, Stan Clarke and others I do not recall, but I believe we were lucky with the visiting musicians, because then we had some big names from the radio – or should I say 'wireless' – names which may not mean much to you, the reader, but to us then they were like today's super pop stars. For instance, The Kenny Baker Dozen and a smaller band of his, The Half Dozen, Chris Barber, Ken Colyer, Alex Welsh, Humphrey Lyttleton (still going as I write), Johnny Dankworth, both with a big band and his famous 'Seven'. To think that then, in the mid to late 1950s Cleo Laine was just a band singer with this band, while now at 70 the pair of them are well-known if not famous all over the world of jazz.

The Strand, as well as holding weekly dances, also booked visiting touring bands, like Mick Mulligan, George Melly, Sid Phillips and many others who are just fond memories. As I write this it makes me realise just how lucky we were, and how unfortunate the teenagers today are in comparison.

The Strand was far from being a den of iniquity as my mother would have had it. She had forbidden me to set foot in the place, which of course had just the opposite effect on me and I went the first chance I got. It was really quite respectable, except for the odd night when the American forces paid a visit and there happened to be one or two National Service squaddies in who might have taken umbrage at the Yanks trying, and often succeeding, to pinch their girls. Then it could be like a scene from a John Wayne movie, as the fights broke out, but these were few and far between.

The Strand was run, maybe even owned, by one Les Birch, who also ran the school of dancing there, and it was so well organised that private coaches were laid on to get everyone home after the dance, for something like a shilling, or five pence in decimal coinage, we having made our own way there via a hostelry or two.

These times were obviously where my love of jazz and big band music began, and this has lasted the forty-five years to this day.

Other venues we visited on the occasional coach trip, would be The Sale Locarno, Trentham Gardens Ballroom, the Parr Hall at Warrington and even Blackpool Tower Ballroom. It may seem funny now to need a coach trip to these places, but of course none of us had our own cars then. A few of the lads had motor bikes, but it was a bit difficult to persuade a girl to ride home on the back of a bike when she might have spent a good-ly part of her pay on the latest hairdo.

Because the pay of a apprentice was very low, saving for hol-idays was always difficult: it meant working all the overtime available and just when you needed it the most it stopped; so to try to save on leisure spending, I would stay in. It was not a very bright prospect at the best of times, but now we had T.V. at home I preferred to take a box of my old 78s to Keith Wilding's where his mother welcomed us and allowed us the use of the front room. I have very fond memories of frosty win-

Me aged about 20 years

ter nights, taking turns with Keith, winding up the gramophone and turning over the precious and very fragile records, with a few bottles of Guinness and a couple of pints of bitter from the Church Inn just across the road, listening to Gerry Mulligan playing "Walking shoes" on the reverse was "Lullaby of the leaves", or maybe the latest Ted Heath big band recording. I even had a few of the Nat King Cole trio on twelve-inch 78s, recorded before he became a solo singer.

On one such night, no doubt lulled by the music, the Guinness fill-ups we had consumed and the hissing of the gas fire, we were awakened at about 1.30am by Keith's mum and dad who had been

Me on holiday at Butlins

out dancing. Come to think of it, we might have had a lucky escape from carbon monoxide poisoning. They were simple pleasures by today's standards, but I look back on those cold winter nights with fondness.

Around about 1957 the Soviet Union took the whole world by surprise by announcing that they had launched the world's first artificial satellite, named Sputnik 1. The media had a field day, the Americans had kittens and I had a smug expression on my face for quite some time. The reason for that was that I'd had the 'mickey' taken out of my belief that one day space travel would be possible, and Terry Mears in particular took great delight in goading me, to such an extent that we even came to fisticuffs one day. We were good pals thereafter, and he was big enough to come and admit he was wrong. Now of course not even a Space Shuttle launch can make the front pages unless it goes wrong.

How blasé we have become! To think that as I was growing up even adults would stop and look up at any aircraft flying over, now only the Concorde can produce a result. I hope I never get so uninterested as that in my surroundings.

Not all my spare time was spent in dance halls though, as I've said, money was scarce and so we had to find other cheaper pastimes. Some evenings if the weather was fine we would take off for a walk, as often as not though we would end up in a pub playing darts. One of our favourite haunts was The Talbot, gone now to make room for the row of shops opposite Dixons, on which site was another nice pub, The George and Dragon – or maybe it would be a game of snooker in the old Gladstone Club next to the Brunner Library, destroyed by fire in the early 1970s, unfortunately.

At this point I suppose I had better tell you a bit about some of my friends. We were, still are really, known as Big John Stanley, Little John Higgins, Big Mike Kearnen, Little Mike Naughton, Big Pete ('yours truly') and Little Pete Treasure. This combination caused a few smiles when we would go into a pub, because everyone was ordering pints of bitter, mixed, black and tans, etc., except Big Mike, who only drank orange juice, and sometimes had a bit of difficulty persuading the person behind the bar that he was serious, that is until one memorable night in the Old Broken Cross, where we had gone for just one before having an early night, and Big Mike, ordering last as usual, asked for a pint of bitter or mild – I was too astonished to remember, it might just as well have been a pint of hemlock for the effect it had on all present – so that was not an early night after all, indeed it was quite a good time had by all.

Although, by this time, we had T.V. at home, I took little interest in it. Not much has changed there you may say – well, there was very little to interest me, as there was only one channel then, the B.B.C. and only in black and white on the old 425 lines system. The picture was not too good either, so once the novelty had worn off, I preferred the good old steam radio. *The Goon Show* was my favourite, and even then there were a few good music programmes, but my favourite stations then were American Forces Network (A.F.N.) and The Voice of America (V.O.A.), which were broadcasting from Stuttgart to all the U.S.

I looked a real swell in my best suit!

forces in Europe together with a bit of anti-communist propaganda. This was still during the Cold War, when many people thought it was just a matter of time before the Russians or the Americans would start throwing nuclear weapons at each other – thankfully they did not.

The signature tune for V.O.A. then was Duke Ellington's own signature tune, *Take the 'A' Train*. The first time I heard this number I was hooked on The Duke and have been ever since. I believe he was the best jazz musician ever, and the best composer too of this century in my humble opinion.

I had many other favourites, Count Basie, Woody Herman, Benny Goodman, Louis Armstrong, and our own Ted Heath and Jonny Dankworth. By now I had my own radio in the bedroom I shared with my brother Robert, an old valve 'steam radio', as the Goons would say. It had a beautiful tone and took a about a minute to warm up, and I would spend many an evening listening to the two hours of jazz from eight to ten in a unheated room.

As well as playing jazz, the Americans also played a good deal of what was pop then, maybe 'popular' would be a better description, stars like Ella Fitzgerald, Nat King Cole, Sarah Vaughn and many more. Imagine my shock and disappointment when I returned to Britain after my National Service, to switch on V.O.A. and hear Rock 'n' Roll! I felt betrayed. That's the price of progress, I suppose.

133

Mum and Dad all dressed up for my wedding

Because clothes and fashion seem to obsess many people today, it seems only proper that I give an idea of how we dressed then. Jeans and tee-shirts and ankle length baseball boots (these were as popular with us as trainers are today), were favourites, but only for relaxing in, no one would dream of 'going out' in them, not even to the pub. I very much doubt if you would have been allowed into a dance hall in jeans, and even to go to the cinema people dressed 'properly', by that I mean in a jacket, slacks, tie, and not until the latter part of the 1950s did you go to a dance in anything but a suit and tie.

And then came the Edwardian style, the 'Teddy Boys', who must have spent a small fortune on their suits with the drainpipe trousers, fully draped jackets with their velvet collars, and string ties, and I have to say, they really did look smart. Not all the 'Teds' were trouble-makers, why spend all that money on clothes only to ruin them in a fight? Some were, of course, but these were in the minority, but because a few had gained notoriety in gang fights with cut-throat razors and bike chains, unfortunately every one dressed in the Edwardian style was tarred with the same brush.

The first suit I had made for myself at Lunns Tailors caused a bit of a rumpus at home, because my dad thought the trousers were too narrow – they were 18 inches at the bottom leg!

Other clothes were Slim Jim ties, so called because they were very narrow, and Sloppy Joe sweaters. Tony Curtis, crew cut and "D.A.' hair styles also caused a bit of a stir, so I suppose I'm following a tradition in criticising styles of today.

All I remember of the clothes girls wore were the flared skirts and blouses or tight sweaters which they often wore a very broad belt – anyway I was too busy admiring the contents to bother about the wrapping!

Like most of my peers I enjoyed a pint or two, and in those unenlightened days, enjoyed a smoke, which I now freely admit was a waste of hard-earned money. We had not then had the health warnings, although the research must have been going on at the time.

During this period of my teenage years as I've already said, I became increasingly interested in GIRLS, females of the opposite sex. And I had some very nice girl friends, none of them too serious, until on New Year's Eve 1956, John Higgins and I made a half-serious bet, as to who would get the most girl friends in the next year, 1957, the rules being that each one would have to last for at least two weeks, and include a minimum of four dates, I think. I believe it was neck and neck (no pun intended) until April, when I met Freda Acton, who was to become my wife. This has lasted for 42 years up to the time of writing. John won the bet,

Freda Acton, about 1957

135

'Little Pete' Treasure and 'Big John' Stanley pictured with me when Freda and I got married

just, as he also met his future wife.

Apparently Freda and I had met on a coach trip to Blackpool Illuminations the previous Autumn, but I don't remember this.

Because we were seeing each other such a lot, this clearly meant a change to my socialising, and meant I would only be going out with "the boys" once or twice a week. Thursday nights were almost always the Talbot Inn, mentioned earlier, to play darts, drink a pint or two, and chat a lot. This was a very good pub for us because when the darts team were playing in the bar, and we were playing in the back room, we would always get a share of the pies and sandwiches which were brought round by the landlord's wife, whose name eludes me at the moment.

If we were not playing darts, then it would be snooker at The Gladstone Club. The steward here was Fred Peak, who had a daughter, Dorothy who became a friend later in life.

Life went on very nicely for a while. There was still not much money, but we made the most of what we had, even enough for a holiday at Billy Butlin's Pwelli holiday camp. Now of course, a holiday with your girl/boy friend, is taken for granted, but this was not the case with us, though I have to say Freda's parents were very good and treated us as adults. John Higgins was not so fortunate and Beryl's mother took much persuading. Both Freda and I had to be vetted by her, but we won her over in the end.

In August 1959, I was declared redundant by Yarwoods. I had already had my National Service medical at Liverpool, where, after much coughing, peeing, bending, eye testing, etc., I was declared 'A1, fit as a fiddle', this despite having a badly damaged left eye. For the next nine weeks I lived off the dole and charity, until I was invited to be the guest of Her Majesty at Catterick Camp, and so it was that, on 5 November 1959, I waited with two more Yarwoods lads, Reg Mayo and Edgar Thompson, on a bleak Northwich railway station... and that's another chapter.

THE YOUNG FIREMAN'S TALE:
The last days of steam

BRUCE FISHER

The author and his family originally came from Bromley-by-Bow in East London, where his father was a engine driver and his brother a fireman at Devons Road Locomotive Shed. Devons Road was the first British Railways depot to be fully dieselised in 1958 but in 1963 the company decided to close it down. Everyone was offered employment at other depots and his father and brother accepted jobs at Northwich. His father had already booked him an interview with the railway and he got a job immediately.

Northwich locomotive depot stood next to Northwich station and the entrance was via a footpath from Middlewich Road. The site has now been developed for housing and a car wash.

Engine Cleaner

I was fifteen years old when I started work as an engine cleaner at Northwich Motive Power Depot. It was a completely different world – only weeks before I had been a pupil at school in East London, living with my grandmother in Mile End until I finished my schooling. British Railways had many domestic properties before they started selling off their housing stocks, and we had been allocated a railway cottage in Hodge Lane, Hartford. Brian Webb, a passed fireman at the depot, lived with his family two doors down from us at No 1. Wilf Ainsworth, a foreman platelayer on the top CLC line, lived with his family at No 2. We lived at No 3. Danny Maxted, a foreman platelayer on the bottom LMS line, lived with his wife at No 4. Platelayers were the guardians of the track, carrying out the daily checks and maintenance of the track and trackside. They all had a pride in their own section and were often seen out with their scythes cutting down the rough grass and saplings on the banks.

On my first day at work, I reported to the office and was told to wait in the cabin for the storeman. The cabin was quite spacious inside with six tables against the right hand wall. A large gas urn was bubbling away on a bench next to a sink against the other wall. In the middle of the cabin stood a cast iron stove, in the winter it would glow red sending out enough heat to warm a cabin four times the size, but at the moment it was a resting place for someone's billycan. A door at the end led to a locker room. There were two tables in the room and it was used as a rest room for the cleaners and labourers.

In the main room a dozen or so enginemen sat about, some playing cards, some drinking tea and chatting. Luckily Brian Webb was on his break and I joined him for a brew.

The storeman, Austin Dutton, took me to an old wheel-less carriage that was the clothing stores. He supplied me with the familiar bib and brace overalls, jackets, and the plastic topped hat. Then I was introduced to the other cleaners in the back room of the cabin and sent off to clean my first engine.

To clean an engine we had to get some rags and a mixture of oil and paraffin from the stores. We had to rub the mixture onto the paintwork making sure that any thick oil deposits and grime were removed before wiping off the oil leaving the black paintwork shining. Sometimes the job was not done as it should have been. One day we just sloshed the mixture over the engine and went to hide and play cards in an old carriage on the back road. The engine went out on the local tripper and on its first trip back it was covered in dandelion seeds that had stuck to the oil. The foreman, Dick Irving, was not very happy with us.

Cleaners were sometimes used for 'knocking up'. That meant getting on the depot bicycle and delivering slips for change of duty, rest day work, etc. It was not a bad job but could get tedious, especially if you had one call at the pre-fabs in Marbury and another in Winsford.

Cleaners were also used as labourers if there was too much work for the shed labourers to do. It was good to go labouring as the rate of pay was almost double that of cleaning. Most of the time labouring you would be shovelling ashes out of the ash pit between the rails onto the trackside, then from the trackside up onto a wagon. This job was quite unpleasant if a fire had just been dropped, for all the fumes and ash would choke you. But it was better than cleaning and a lot of the ashes were old and damp anyway.

Another labouring job was drying the sand and filling the sand bin. The sand used to come in open trucks, and it had to be shovelled up through an opening in the side of the sand shed, then into a hopper that was built around a small furnace.

My father in engine number 43024 at Devons Road depot in 1952. In the photo you can see the sand delivery pipes forward and reverse on the centre driving wheel and forward on the front driving wheel.

When the sand was dry a trap was opened at the bottom and the sand ran out into a barrow. It was then wheeled round to the engine shed and shovelled into a bin ready for the fireman to top up the sand box on each side of the engine before leaving the shed.

The sand was used to give extra grip under the driving wheels, to prevent them slipping when pulling away. The sanders were controlled by a valve in the cab: a steam jet caused a vacuum in the sand pipe, drawing the sand into the pipe and forcibly blowing it out through a nozzle under the tread of the driving wheels.

Finally there was another labouring job, usually on the afternoon or night shift. If a coal stage worker did not turn up for work the shed firemen and labourers could and usually would refuse to cover for them, so it was left to the cleaners. The coal was shovelled out of trucks into square bins which were lifted by crane and tipped into the tenders by the shedmen. You could have an easy day if there weren't many engines about. But most of the time they would be lined up one after the other and it was very hard work.

I was also getting settled outside work. My brother took me to meet his friends in the Bridge Café in the Bull Ring. It was quite a popular place for the local teenagers, as was the coffee bar further up town on the corner of Meadow Street, and both places stayed open till late at night. I soon got to know all the regulars in the Bridge Café, especially Jackie. I had of course kissed girls before but only brief hurried kisses.

Jackie showed me what a proper passionate kiss was and it blew my socks off!

Although most young people spoke with a general northern accent, there were still a large amount of older people in the area who spoke with the old Cheshire dialect. It was a treat to listen to them talking, even if sometimes I had difficulty understanding some of the phrases. Sadly the dialect is rarely heard nowadays.

I had started drifting from The Bridge Café up to the back room of The Crown for a game of darts, a pasty, and a pint. Lenny Heywood was a bit older than me and was quite a good dart thrower. He also held the record for dropping a pint of beer, in seconds. I thought I'd be able to do that one day, but the only way I could drop a pint that fast was if I dropped it onto the floor. Lenny worked at Bates' Iron Foundry and was respected by the local lads. Just being in his company stopped me from getting a right-hander on a least one occasion. From there I started calling at The Fox, just behind the Old Market Hall.

There was a group of older girls who always seemed to be in there. It was all right if I were with some lads, but if I were on my own they would have great fun pretending to chat me up, using some quite lewd innuendoes, and laughing at my embarrassment. I was often relived to see some of my friends walk in. My days at The Fox came to an abrupt end when the friendly local police sergeant collared me – I was still only fifteen.

The summonses soon arrived, one for me and one for my dad. To say that my dad went ballistic would be an understatement, it was his first-ever summons as well as mine.

Passed Cleaner

Eventually I was sent with two other cleaners to the firing school in Speke. Two weeks later we took the test and two of us, Ken Syson and myself, passed. We were not yet graded as firemen. We were 'passed cleaners', which meant that although we were still cleaners we were available for firing duties if required.

Back at Northwich we started our third man duties on the steam engines. This was basically 'in service' training on the local trippers and the fireman was there to show you the job.

There were two trippers at Northwich with two shifts — morning and afternoon – working each one. The trippers could do three trips in a shift. One worked from Northwich sidings up the Arches, then just before Greenbank the line branched off to the right, then crossed over Chester Road by the Thatched Tavern and dropped down into Oakleigh sidings next to Verdin Park and Northwich Infirmary. *(The track in Oakleigh sidings has now been taken up, only a direct route through to Winnington Works remains.)*

The other tripper worked from Northwich sidings up the Arches, through Greenbank, branching right at Hartford Junction (Cheshire Lines), under the bridge at Hodge Lane, past Hartford Junction (LMS) and into Wallerscote sidings between Weaverham and the main line from London to Scotland.

The sidings have now been dismantled. (The dismantled private I.C.I. mineral railway from Wallerscote sidings to Wallerscote works passes under Northwich Road between Hartford and Weaverham.)

The first day was magic. Although it was only local work we were pulling full train loads with a Class 8 engine. The trip engine was also used as a banking engine, pushing the hopper trains to Oakleigh from the rear. Wallerscote hoppers did not need a banker but due to the curve and gradient into Oakleigh some assistance was needed with the hopper trains running there. The banker would come up behind the hopper train in the platform at Northwich station but would not be coupled to the train. When it had pushed the train round the curve, the bank engine would drop away and return to Northwich.

At this point I suppose I should describe how a steam engine works, so you will get an idea of what a fireman's job entails.

To power a steam engine, coal is burned in a firebox producing hot gases (mainly carbon dioxide). These gases then heat water in a boiler to produce steam. If the flow of air to the fire is not correct then high levels of harmful carbon monoxide gas are produced as well as black smoke indicating a wasteful loss of available heat. The distinctive dome on top of the engine is the highest and driest part of the boiler and it houses the main internal steam pipe, the steam pipes to the auxiliary fittings in

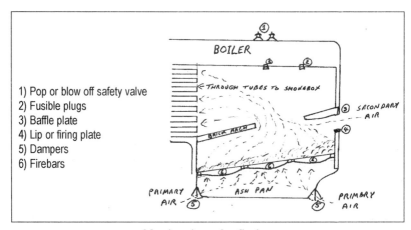

My drawing of a firebox

the cab and the regulator valve. When the regulator is opened by the driver's handle, steam passes through the internal pipe to the super heater header then through the boiler tubes where it is dried and increased in temperature: superheated. When the steam is at high pressure it is fed into the cylinders. The steam expands and forces pistons back and forth, which turns the locomotive's wheels via a rod and crank. When the steam has done its job it is exhausted out into the atmosphere through the funnel, causing a draught through the firebox and drawing the fire.

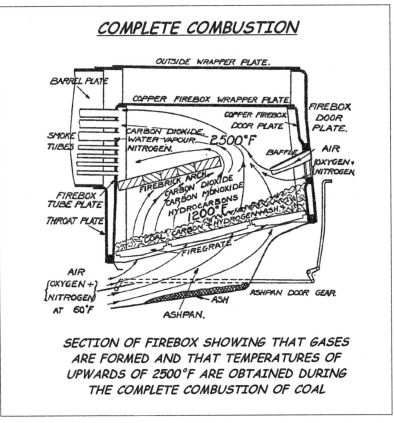

From L.M.S. Railway Company drawings taken from "Questions for Enginemen" (published in 1941).

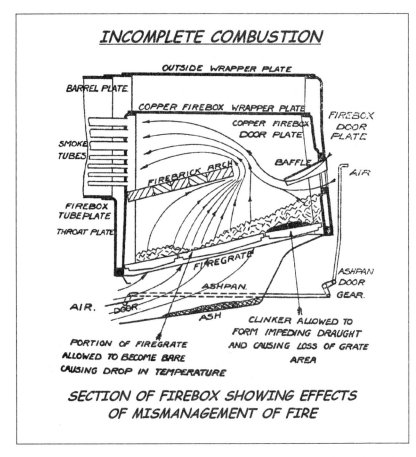

INCOMPLETE COMBUSTION

SECTION OF FIREBOX SHOWING EFFECTS OF MISMANAGEMENT OF FIRE

From L.M.S. Railway Company drawings taken from "Questions for Enginemen" (published in 1941).

There were two injectors on the engine. The injectors were used as a means of transferring water from the tender into the boiler. Steam was used to draw the water by creating a vacuum. The water was then propelled under steam pressure through a valve and into the boiler. One injector was a live steam injector. The other worked off the exhaust steam when the locomotive was running under power, reverting to using live steam when the locomotive was not running under power. It was therefore more practical to use the exhaust injector than the live steam injector.

I got my first firing turn straight after finishing third man duty. I signed on, checked my engine number, 48640, then walked round to the engine stores. I was issued with a firing shovel, a coal pick, a bucket of spanners and detonators, two headlamps, and a gauge lamp. The lamps had to be checked for paraffin, good wicks, and a red shade, because our relief could be out after dark.

When I got to the engine, the driver Dennis Lewis was busily oiling the side rods. I exchanged the usual "Hello mate," with him and climbed aboard. After putting all the tools in their places and my lunchbag in the locker, I pulled the dart out of the tender and spread the fire before shovelling some more coal into the firebox. The dampers were open, and the blower jet was on slightly, drawing the fire nicely.

There was plenty of steam and the boiler was full. We had a good one – it looked as if the engine had just come in off a run and had been dealt with by the shedmen so it had not been at the mercy of the steam raisers overnight. Now just a quick look in the back of the tender was needed to check that the water gauge was working, then it was off to the sand bin to get a bucket of sand to fill the engine sand boxes.

We set off from the shed tender first and travelled the short distance to the sidings. The guard hooked up and chatted to the driver then walked off down the train. I'd got quite a lot of coal on now with the dampers shut and the jet on slightly, the coal was burning well sending a black plume of smoke from the funnel. The driver stood up and filled his cup from the billycan sitting on the tray above the fire-hole doors. Before he sat back down he casually opened the doors and eased on the blower jet slightly to disperse the smoke.

Off came the signal and I opened the dampers as the driver lifted the regulator and we started to pull away. My driver told me to watch for a wave from the guard to make sure he was aboard. Sure enough there he was waving a white rag from the brake van, a quick pop on the whistle and he disappeared from view.

The draught through the fire had brought it fully to life and it was roaring as the driver lifted the regulator higher. The safety blow-off valves on top of the engine burst into action sending two jets of steam skyward. I knocked on the injector, the boiler looked full but I didn't want to waste any more of the steam. A little more coal, the safety valves stopped blowing, I turned the injector off, shut the firebox doors and sat on the small wooden drop-down seat.

We went roaring into Northwich station like a big black monster. As I looked out of the window I noticed two girls sitting on a bench by the ticket office. I gave a pop on the whistle and waved. The girls waved back, it was something to do with the whistle – a pop or blast on the whistle and they would always wave back! Under the road bridge then I was up again to put some more coal on. We passed over the Arches, and still pounding forcefully we turned off the main line, round the curve, over the Iron Bridge by the Thatched Tavern and started to drop down into Oakleigh sidings.

The regulator was closed and the boiler gauge glass was showing half full. I turned on the injector to stop the safety valves blowing, but because we were going downhill and getting a false reading from the gauge I had to be very careful not to overfill the boiler. I looked in at the fire which was burning down nicely. My first trip was over, almost perfect. But I had been lucky. I had a good engine and a very good driver. I could only hope now for a bit of experience before getting the bad ones.

Passing For Main Line – first attempt

I was booked on with the firing inspector from Liverpool to pass for main line work. It was usual to work a train up the bank to Godley, east of Hyde in Greater Manchester. But the train had been cancelled and we were to work to Dee Marsh steelworks, about six miles the other side of Chester.

The driver was in his fifties and was not of the type that I was used to on the trippers. He was a top link driver and didn't seem to like the idea of lowly me being on his engine.

Let me explain how we were organised and ranked. A "link" was a group of duties. The bottom link, the shed link, had six duties. Passed cleaners who were made up to firemen would start in the shed link. Each week they would follow on the rota from the previous week, with Week 1 following again after Week 6. The next link was the spare link, with a rota of signing-on times to cover holidays, sickness, absenteeism, specials, relief work and so on. The other links were main line jobs and the train crews moved up these links as vacancies arose, eventually arriving in the highest link, the prestigious "top link". The firemen in the top link were mostly passed firemen who could work as drivers when required.

My driver's mate was a passed fireman who seemed to have caught a dose of the miserables off the driver. Neither one spoke as I got onto the footplate, just a nod from the passed fireman as I said 'hello'. The inspector, a tall thin man, was not a beaming delight either, but he was not supposed to be so he couldn't be faulted for that.

All went well at first, I had the boiler full, plenty of steam and enough coal on to allow just a topping up when we were under way. I hoped we wouldn't be delayed in starting because although the dampers were closed, it would not take long for the fire to burn up causing the safety valves to blow off wastefully. The signal went up and we were off. Out through Northwich station and up over the Arches, this bit was of course easy, I had done it many times on the trippers. Up past the branch to Wallerscote sidings and the bottom line – the main line to Liverpool and Scotland. We had passed all the places that I had been used to and were still climbing. It was just before Delamere station that I started having trouble. I couldn't raise the steam pressure. I wasn't losing any steam through the working of the train, but every time I put on the injector to fill the boiler I lost steam pressure which I couldn't seem to make up. Just past Delamere the pressure had dropped quite a lot. We were not in serious trouble yet, but I didn't think it would be very long until we were. I shovelled even more coal on, trying to see if I had missed a patch in the firebed. It was now full as I could get it while still allowing the heat to circulate. I could not get any more coal in without overfilling the box. I slammed the firebox doors shut – that should do it, I thought.

Almost immediately the driver shut off the regulator, we had started downhill. I looked over to the driver but he was looking outside, as was the passed fireman. I looked at the inspector and shook my head, but he appeared to be uninterested in my gesture. The needle on the steam pressure gauge was moving up fast now, almost as fast as the seconds hand on an electric clock. I knocked the injector on and eased the dampers down, but it wasn't long before the boiler safety valves blew and kept on blowing. I tried to turn the other injector on but couldn't get it to work. We were still dropping downhill and it would be a few miles before we would start on the rising gra-

Ken Syson and myself skylarking

dient through Mickle Trafford.

At last the regulator was opened but not for long as the inspector wanted to get off at the small branch that led to Chester Northgate station. I got off with him and walked up to the station. The engine was still blowing off as it went out of sight, like it had been all the way from Mouldsworth.

I had of course failed, but the inspector told me it wasn't a big problem and we would try again in a few weeks. It was strange to hear someone speak. The driver and passed fireman although speaking to each other and the inspector occasionally, had not said a word to me all the time that I had been on the engine. I got on the passenger train back to Northwich feeling as if I too had caught a dose of the miserables.

Pilot

It was the pilot's job to shunt the goods yard (where Tesco now is). It also shunted Park's steelworks (now B&Q) and did trips to Marston and Winsford salt works.

The engine on this job was a small Class 2 tender engine, 46487. It had a very small firebox and was a lovely engine to work on.

My driver, Bill Elson, didn't seem to have a care in the world and would not rush for anyone. The guards and shunters knew this and would never ask him to hurry up, because they knew that if they did he would go even slower. He was a pleasant jovial man who took no interest in the firing side as long as he thought that the fireman could cope. He just wanted to drive the train, smoke his pipe and drink tea. So different from a lot of drivers who thought that their fireman didn't have a clue how to do the job. We were doing little shunting jobs all morning with quite a lot of standing time. As this was an engine that never went to another depot, it was usual for the fireman to polish up the brasses on the footplate, something rarely done on the Class 8's. The engine looked a treat.

In the afternoon we left with half a dozen empty salt trucks for Winsford. Up over the Arches chugging away like Ivor The

Engine. It was a nice sunny lazy summer's day and it made a change from belting up here on the trippers. We carried on up the bank through Greenbank, past Cuddington station and turned off onto the Winsford branch line. The branch line was a single track running through a mainly wooded area. The young trees were growing right up to the track and there were even plants growing between the sleepers. I was fascinated – it was like a scene from a wild west movie. We passed a long dis-used station at Whitegate then further on a small level cross-ing. The crossing keeper lived in a house by the crossing and I think that he must have been semi-retired as there were only two trains a week down this branch line.

We dropped down towards Winsford and crossed the road into the I.C.I. salt-mine works. After a bit of shunting we set off with our loaded salt trucks tender-first to Northwich. We stopped at the crossing keeper's house and he transferred a fresh pot of tea into our billycan. The usual dozen or so shov-els of coal fell off the engine and landed next to his coal-shed.

We were soon back at Northwich, but before going home I stopped for refreshment in the railwaymen's main rest room, in the back room of The Lion and Railway Hotel. The bar was quite busy when I walked in. Shunters, guards and train crews all used it. It was unusual to see someone in the bar who was not a serving or retired railway worker. They'd be there before work, after work and even during breaks – purely for refresh-ment of course, for nobody could afford to be caught drunk on duty.

I noticed four strangers playing cards at one of the tables. They were 'foreigners', train crews from other depots, maybe Birkenhead, Stoke, Liverpool or a host of other places, passing time while waiting to relieve their return trains.

Two firemen, Les Hitchens and Kenny Edwards, were play-ing darts in the recess that seemed to have been built just for the purpose. I joined them for a few games but after two pints of bitter I had to leave. I was only young and had to cycle home, so any more would have been a mistake.

After leaving the bar I made good progress wobbling home on my bicycle, but the hill at Castle was looming up in front of me. I got halfway up, struggling and about to give up, when the Broadhurst bus went past. All the curler-headed factory girls were waving at me from the windows. I had to carry on, couldn't look weak in front of the girls.

Godley (first main line turn)

A fireman failed to turn in for the morning run up to Godley sidings. I had worked with the driver, Ernie Southern, four times on the trippers, and we'd had no problems. I was the only passed cleaner available to cover the turn, but as I was not passed for main line the driver had to be asked if he were prepared to take me. He was of course well within his rights to refuse. I was a little worried in case he did refuse, especially as it was common knowledge that I had failed the main line test and I was pleasantly surprised when he said that he had no problems with my firing ability and was perfectly willing to have me as his fireman. There were many different types of drivers. Some of them could make the fireman's job quite hard, but Ernie was one of the drivers that through the best use of the controls made the engine do most of the work, and I've never known him to use the second regulator position unnecessarily.

We left the shed with a Class 8 engine, 48528, and made our way to the top end sidings. I was very eager to go, even though I'd been told it was quite a hard slog up the bank from Stockport to Godley. We set off with a mixed train of covhops, vans, and some finished steel that had been brought forward from Dee Marsh steelworks. Ernie was keeping an eye on my firing and was advising me all the way, as well as doing his own job. This was the first time I had been in this direction and I was as grateful for his guidance as I was for his faith in my ability. After all, if I messed up, it would be him that would have to carry the can.

Through Knutsford, Altrincham, then via Skelton Junction to Stockport. My first trip up the bank from Stockport to Godley was, as I had been told, a long hard slog and I wondered if it would ever come to an end. But we made it to the top with no problems at all. We dropped our train in the sidings and made our way to the turntable where we turned the engine before taking our meal break. I felt terrific and was eager to pick up our train for the journey back to Northwich, feeling that I could now tackle anything.

Clockface

I was on nights, when there was a good chance of firing work as there were not many cleaners on nights. Again a fireman failed to turn up, this time for the Clockface run, and I was the only passed cleaner available for firing. The driver had to be asked if he was prepared to take me. My father was the driver so there was no problem!

We set off from the sidings with our soda ash, covered hoppers ('covhops') for Pilkington's Glass Works. Out via Hartford Junction and onto the bottom line, through to Runcorn, over the Mersey bridge and down into the sidings at Widnes. There was a brake van at either end of the train and we changed ends and went tender-first from here to Saint Helens. The run to Saint Helens was as you can imagine – very dusty with all the coal dust from the tender being blown onto the footplate – but at least it wasn't raining. We arrived at the sidings and the inevitable "brew up, mate!" echoed across the cab. I set off to the shunters' cabin to perform the most important task of the night. We had our break then turned the engine on the triangle for the trip tender-first back to Widnes, then engine-first to Northwich. On the way over the Mersey bridge I had my first driver training spell, but not for long as I was a bit heavy-handed and my Dad had visions of having to unwrap the guard from around the stovepipe in the brake van.

Pickup

The pickup must be one of the oldest jobs at the shed. At one time all the stations had their own goods yards. It was the pickup's job to shunt these yards. I was booked on with Doug Sunderland and we had a Class 8, No. 48500. We shunted the yards up to Knutsford in the morning and the yards to Mouldsworth in the afternoon. There was not much to do at the stations, for the vans and trucks for local deliveries stopped before I started work here. It was just a matter of shunting the few trucks for the coalmen and the ballast wagons for the Permanent Way staff who maintained the track.

(The 'Permanent Way' is a finished road bed of rails, fittings, sleepers and ballast. The name dates from the days of the railway builders when "permanent way" was used to distinguish a finished job from the "temporary way" used during construction.)

(During my time at Northwich these goods yards closed down one by one.)

My Generation

Pop music seemed to be a major influence in the sixties. A transition from the ballads of the fifties, first the American rock'n'roll, then the explosion of sounds from Merseyside. Many stars from the hit parade performed at The Memorial Hall, generally known as "The Morgue". On Saturday nights the place would attract young people from miles around, filling the nearby Penrhyn Arms to capacity prior to the start of the evening's entertainment. I only went to The Morgue a couple of times to see The Hollies and The Merseybeats. I preferred the pubs, thinking The Hall was for dancers, not drinkers, and I thought I was a drinker. I spent a lot of time in the Penrhyn Arms, but my time there ran out when my old friend the police sergeant collared me again, almost a year after The Fox.

The Beatles performed at The Memorial Hall before we moved here, but my wife Sheila went to watch them, and remarks on how she queued for three hours for a ticket. She also saw them at The Cavern and The Pavilion at New Brighton. There were always coaches going to other dance

My wife Sheila's early dancing days with a troupe at Greenbank in the early fifties.

halls, especially when the Memorial Hall was not open. Unlike me, Sheila was a dancer, not a drinker, and was a dance student at Kitty Oakes dance studio across from the old Northwich bus terminus.

Passing For Main Line – second attempt

At last the footplate inspector had arrived for my second attempt at passing for main line. I was feeling quite confident. I'd had a lot more experience and had already been to Godley, but I was not so confident when I got my engine number, 92053, a big black Class 9. I had never fired a Class 9 and I had visions of another failure. These engines had ten driving wheels instead of the eight driving wheels on the Class 8's. All the controls were different, and although the firebox was short-er, it was much wider.

We set off for Godley. I had worked with the driver, Doug Sunderland, on the pickup so we were not footplate strangers. He was completely different from the one on the previous test and was telling me in good time when he would be shutting off or opening up as well as other bits of advice. The inspector didn't seem to mind this and we arrived at Godley without a hitch. The inspector told me I had passed, said his 'cheerios' then set off down the sidings to who knows where.

Chester Passenger

Sometimes, due to breakdowns there were not enough diesel multiple units (D.M.U.s) to cover all the services between Manchester Central and Chester Northgate so steamers had to be used.

It was early evening as I walked across to Northwich station with Frank Sissons to relieve the passenger train to Chester. I noticed the sudden excitement as the people waiting on the platform were pleasantly surprised by the sight of the steamer approaching with five old carriages. It drew up to the end of the platform bang on time. Steaming and squeaking it came to a halt. It was a Class 5 45393. Because it had just come down the bank from Knutsford it had a full boiler and a full head of steam. The previous fireman had put some coal on, but I put some more on for the climb up the Arches to our first stop at Hartford & Greenbank. The safety valves on top of the boiler erupted sending a plume of steam forcefully skyward as we got the whistle from the guard to get going. The driver had to get the train moving as quickly as possible and as we passed through the bridge at the end of the platform he put it into full power (second regulator), but he was a bit too eager and the wheels started to spin, clanking the side rods and sending great embers out of the funnel. He eased back on the power, the wheels gripped the rails and we were soon picking up speed. We were travelling at full power on the gradient out of town and I knew that I wouldn't spend much time sitting on the wooden seat. As we approached the Arches I looked over the River Dane, day-dreaming about my girlfriend Jane. I turned round when I heard Frank shouting and saw him frantically pointing to the boiler gauge glass. I calmly knocked on the water injector then opened the firebox doors. I looked at the swirling mass of yellow and orange flames, then picked up the firing shovel and began to hurl coal into the mouth of the hungry engine.

I gave a blast on the whistle as we approached the cottages at Hodge Lane. I would always give a whistle when passing on the top CLC line or on the branch to Wallerscote. If my mother was in, she would always appear at the back door, along with any visitors that we had at the time, and give a wave. But this time seemed special, hurtling up the bank in the early evening darkness, hauling a passenger train.

We had the four small stations to stop at, Hartford & Greenbank, Cuddington, Delamere and Mouldsworth, and although it needed a fair steam effort to get moving again, the couple of minutes at the stations gave me time to make up any deficiencies. We were travelling very fast and the 'little and often' rule certainly applied. As soon as I had put the shovel down and sat on the seat, I had to get up again.

We pulled into Chester Northgate station *(where the Northgate Arena now stands),* and all the carriage doors started to open. The people were smiling, it had been a treat for them to be on a steam train instead of the usual boring D.M.U.s. As the passengers passed on their way out, I got onto the platform to change the lamps for the light engine trip back to Northwich. I couldn't help feeling a little proud to be the fireman, the star of the show.

Hoppers

A diesel shortage again, but this time it was the type two hopper engine. The brakes were modified on these engines and they couldn't be replaced by a normal Type 2, so whenever there was a shortage, steamers were used. I had already worked on a hopper train with a Class 9 engine, but we got relief when we returned to Northwich. My next trip was with the normal Class 8, and we worked through to Oakleigh.

I was booked on with George Blease, engine number 48073. A spare crew had been up to the I.C.I. sidings and picked up the train. We relieved them at the end of the platform at

Me pictured by a Class 8 (Sheila's Yorkie has devoured the bottom of the photo!)

Northwich station and set off for Peak Forest. We headed towards Cheadle on the same line as the Godley traffic. Once you got to Cheadle you turned off onto the main line to Buxton then start the long climb though Disley and Chapel-en-le-Frith to the works at Peak Forest. It was as expected a long hard slog, but my driver would take the shovel now and then to give me a rest. We had our break at the top then backed onto our train for our return trip. This time the hoppers were loaded with limestone and were very heavy. The train was fitted with vacuum brakes from front to back, but even this would not stop the train if it were going too fast, so the driver had to be very cautious on the way down. It was rumoured that it was not unknown for these trains to pass a red signal.

We had a short hard stretch under power from the sidings, then over the top and the long descent down to Cheadle. Back under power through to Altrincham and up the bank past Knutsford and over the M6 then down to Northwich.

We were supposed to pull into the platform for relief and to allow the banker to come behind, but we were turned into the loop at the sidings. A shunter said that there was no relief and asked if we would work through to Oakleigh. The driver was quite happy to continue, and so was I.

The signal came off and we dropped down to the signal in the station platform to await the banking engine. The fire was built up and the engine had just started to blow off as the banker came behind. I knew we wouldn't be kept waiting long as we were a top priority train. Off came the signal. I gave a whistle to the banker as my driver took the brakes off. The banker whistled back and we felt a surge of power from behind. I saw the great fountain of blackish smoke as his wheels slipped a little. My driver opened up and away we went. We were soon going at full power up the Arches. I looked back past the line of uniform hoppers with their limestone crowns, the Class 8 behind working just as hard as us. With all this power we were still slowing down as we went round the curve on the Oakleigh branch. We dropped down into the sidings, the banker made his way back to town and the I.C.I. diesel shunter was waiting to take the train into Winnington works. We ran round the train and shunted the brake van against three or four others before picking up the guard and setting off light engine for the shed.

Winsford was a popular place with a lot of young people from Northwich. The Strand was turning into quite a good nightclub under the Mr Smith's banner, becoming popular because it was the only youngsters' nightclub in the Northwich and Winsford area. There was trouble there sometimes, but it was quite rare compared to a lot of other places, although I

My brother Ian posing on 44766

have seen the place erupt into a violent near riot with bottles, chairs and even tables being thrown between two rival parties. Most of the time though people just enjoyed themselves till two in the morning, drinking, dancing, and flirting.

Socially I was spending a lot of time in Winsford. I was now at the age when I was taking a lot of interest in girls. Especially the two blonde bombshells in their micro skirts and leopard skin bolero jackets. Nice to look at, but don't take them home to meet your Mum.

The Strand has received some bad publicity as being a bit seedy, and sure enough there were mid week "Gentlemen's nights", but at weekends the club gave a great deal of enjoyment to a lot of the local youngsters. There was also the bonus

of Winsford's own pop group, "The Look Twice," who regularly performed at the club led by the talented Vince Wilkinson. Across the road from Smiths were The Ark, The Oak and the nearby Red Lion, which also catered mainly for youngsters with up-to-date juke boxes in all three public houses.

During the day there were alternatives to visiting the bars. From Wharton Hill over the Weaver bridge on the left there was a row of shops including a small cafe that was used as a meeting place. On hot summer days it was just a short trip from there to the open air swimming pool at Rilshaw Lane. A swim, a bit of horseplay, or just lazing in the sun on the grass overlooking the flashes – many happy hours were spent at the pool in Winsford. It's sad that no trace of the cafe, Mr Smith's or the pool can be found, as if they never existed. The pubs are still there though, but they have been extensively altered.

Tragedy at Acton Grange

The old Clockface run that went via the Runcorn bridge to St Helens had been rerouted via Warrington. On Friday 13 May 1966 a Northwich crew left Wallerscote sidings for the Ravenhead glass works. The goods train consisted of a Class 8 steam locomotive, number 48717, pulling 31 wagons (30 soda ash covhops and a vanfit) and a brake van. The estimated total weight of the train was 1,125 tons.

The 20.40 Euston to Stranraer express was following as the goods train made its way up the bank at Acton Grange near Warrington, crewed by Carlisle staff, and powered by English Electric 2,000 HP diesel engine number D322. The train conveyed 10 vehicles including two sleeper cars and three parcel vans and was estimated at 342½ tons.

Due to a problem with the screw coupling the goods train became detached. The first portion of the train, the engine and two wagons, travelled forward to Walton New Junction. The rear portion, 29 wagons and a brake van, ran away back down the gradient in the wrong direction colliding with the Stranraer express at 23.58, blocking the up and down lines to Crewe.

The Northwich goods guard applied his brakes and jumped clear from his van just before the point of impact. Thirteen cov-hops and the brake van were de-railed; the engine of the express was also de-railed, the front cab flattened by the impact. Four passengers were taken to hospital for minor injuries, but tragically the express train crew were killed.

The emergency services were alerted at 23.59 and the first ambulance arrived at 00.12. The fire brigade arrived at 00.18 and extinguished a fire on the diesel engine. An amount of repairs were needed to the damaged track, but trains were running under caution from 06.30 on Sunday, and normal working resumed on the line at 12.30 on Sunday.

Dee Marsh

On a routine trip to Dee Marsh, I had a passed fireman, Roy Holland, as a driver. The engine however was a bit strange to me. It was called a Crab, 42782, not a large engine, a little smaller than a Class 5. We left Northwich sidings and had only got to the Arches when I knew we were going to have trouble. I was fighting to keep up the steam pressure, and losing. The driver was of course a very experienced fireman and he took over the shovel, but he could do no better then me. He checked the fire and could find nothing wrong with the firing. He eased off the power as much as possible, hoping we could get over the top between Delamere and Mouldsworth, but we both knew that we wouldn't make it. At Delamere we were very low on steam, though we were managing to keep the boiler safe we would not have the steam to get over the summit. The driver stopped at the signal box at Delamere station and told the signalman that we were stopping for a "blow up" to raise the steam pressure. We thought that we would have to split the train in the small siding, but the signalman said that there was nothing behind us so we could wait on the main line, as long as we were not too long.

We built up the steam pressure and gave the signalman a pop on the whistle, he waved us on and we set off once more. We started to lose steam again right away, but made it over the top and started on the long downhill run to Barrow. It took a while for the steam to build up again. Although I had the boiler injector turned on, I kept the fire up and the dampers fully open which would soon have had most engines blowing off, but not this one. Through Barrow and on the approach to Mickle Trafford junction we started to run under power again, once we were past the branch to Chester Northgate Station the run was pretty flat through Blacon and Sealand so we knew we would be all right, but the driver still had to take it easy.

When we arrived at Dee Marsh sidings they had a return train for us, but the driver refused to take it. He telephoned control and told them that he would only take the engine light, and was booking it off. We were told to take the engine to Birkenhead, but when we got there they didn't have a replacement so we travelled home on the passenger service. *(The line from Mickle Trafford to Dee Marsh is now closed).*

Most young people in the mid sixties could not afford a car so the next best option was a motorcycle. I bought my first motorcycle from Scotts Motorcycles in Wheelock Street, Middlewich. It was a James 250cc Superswift and was a smart-looking bike. It was not long before I took my test. At that time you met the examiner at the library then went across to Meadow Street. You did the eyesight test then had to drive slowly alongside the examiner as he walked along the street. For the main part of the test you had to ride up Meadow Street, left into Witton Street, High Street through the Bull Ring, into Chester Way and back into Meadow Street. At some time during the circuits the examiner would stand by the kerb and raise his hand which was a signal to do an emergency stop. You then had to turn round and do the circuits the other way until he stopped you in back Meadow Street.

I passed the test, so the first job was to call to see my girl-friend and give her the good news.

Christine was an apprentice hairdresser, she lived in Winsford and worked at a small salon that used to be almost opposite the school on Wharton Road. I think she might have been a little embarrassed when I turned up unannounced to give her the news, but still she was pleased for me. I called back later to give her a lift home – the first legal lift. Helmets were not a problem as at the time as there was no legal require-ment to wear them. Apart from the test, I only wore mine if the weather was bad or if I was going out touring.

So my main pastimes at that time were drinking with the lads, motorcycling and my girlfriend. In that order, which is probably why Christine gave me the elbow and went off with my mate.

Unfortunately drinking and motorcycling do not mix very well and I fell off my bikes on many occasions, but more of that later. Now it's back to work…

Fireman

I was now the senior passed cleaner. A vacancy came up and I moved into the bottom link, the shed link. I was now graded as a fireman, my cleaning and labouring days were over.

Working as a shedman was not a bad job. There were only three shifts, 6am-2pm, 2-10pm, 10pm-6am. They were on a six week rota allowing for different rest days, with two crews on each shift. The duties of the shedmen, apart from shunting the shed, were the cleaning and disposal of the fires, coaling, watering, turning and sometimes preparing the engines.

To clean the fire you need a steel rod with a small spade on the end called a dart, a long flat-ended rake and a pair of tongs. First you used the dart to scrape some fire to the left hand corner beside the firedoor, then the right side was cleaned out and pushed forward. The clean fire was now transferred to the right and the left side was cleaned out. Next you had to clear a space in the middle of the fire, then using the tongs remove four of the firebars. If there was a lot of clinker formed on the bars you would have to break it up first with the dart. Some firemen would clear a space at the side, remove the bars and place them at the side of the firebox, but I always thought that it was better to draw them right out onto the footplate. Next the rake was used to scrape all the ash, clinker and embers into the ash pan, then push it out through the front damper, taking care not to put too much into the ash pan at once, which would cause a blockage. The rake was now withdrawn with care as it was very hot. The fire bars were laid one at a time on the lip plate in the firehole, gripped with the tongs, pushed inside, levelled up and dropped into place. Once all the bars were in, the remaining fire to the right of the doors was spread and topped up to a heap just under the firehole. The front damper had been cleaned out with the rake, while the rear damper was cleaned out with a firing shovel from the trackside.

Now we moved forward to the smoke box. There were two handles on the smoke box door, a screw and a catch. The screw handle was unwound until the catch could be turned, releasing the door. All the black smoke box ash could now be shovelled out into the pit.

Things didn't always go that smoothly, though. If you dropped a firebar into the ash pan you could sometimes have a lot of trouble getting it out. If an engine had been out a long time it could have three, four or more inches of clinker on the bars, sometimes the firebars even fused themselves together, and though most firemen would bring the engines on shed with as little fire as possible, now and then you would get on an engine and find a great roaring fire which made the job difficult and very hot. You would probably have to remove the rake and get another one half way through because it would be red hot and bending. And what a horrible sight to open the smoke box and find it full to the blast ring.

B.R. standards (Class 9's etc,) were a lot easier to dispose. They were fitted with rocking bars. You put a bar into the socket at the trackside and lifted to open the ash pan. Then on the footplate you located the bar into the left socket and moved it backwards and forwards sending all the fire, ash, and clinker straight through into the ash pit. Next you moved the good fire from the right to the left and rocked the other half. Top up the fire, close the ash pan, and that's it. You were booked an hour to dispose an engine whether it was an eight or a nine. A lot of problems and hard work were caused on the rails if the disposal work was not carried out correctly.

Coaling engines at Northwich required three shedmen, one to work the crane, one to stand on top of the engine cab tipping the bins into the tender, and one to hook the bracket onto the bins ready for lifting. The bracket was a piece of steel, horizontal with a vertical arm at each end. At the end of each arm was a hook which went round a short thick bar each side of the bin. These bars were below the centre making the bins top heavy. After the bracket was in place the driver would work the crane pulling the bin forward until it was just about to lift. There was a U-shaped catch on the bin which now had to be lifted on its hinge and dropped into place with a prong either side of the main bracket. It was now lifted and the crane swung manually on its pivot till it reached the top of the tender. The fireman on the cab roof stepped forward onto the steel ridge of the tender and steadied the bin, lined it up and knocked up the U-catch. Being top heavy it would now fall the right way or the wrong way, so as soon as the U-catch was up, a small pull was needed to ensure that the bin tipped towards you. If it did go the wrong way it could tip half the contents back onto the coal stage, which would send the other shedmen running, and the labourers who filled the bins would not be amused either. As the bin started tipping towards you, you had to step back onto the cab roof to avoid the odd rogue piece of coal hitting your feet. It was usual to put four or five bins into a tender, though some required a lot more.

All the jobs on the shed had a set time, except for shunting, so if there were plenty of engines on the shed, you could all get stuck in, get your day's work done and go home early. Also once you proved yourself capable there were plenty of opportunities for driving, even if it was only on the shed roads.

The Big Bang

One Friday I had to drop the fire on an engine that was not going to be used for a few days. Dropping the fire as opposed to cleaning the fire meant removing all the fire from the firebox. I finished off the job as the rest of the shed men made their way to the cabin for our twenty minute break.

The job had been left a bit late due to other work and the steam pressure was very low so I had to get the engine parked on the back road as soon as possible while I still had the pressure to move the engine.

I opened the regulator, but the engine would not move. I moved the regulator handle further up and eventually the engine began to move very slowly towards the off-shed signal.

As the engine was approaching the points lever for the back road, I would wind the control into reverse gear then drop off the steps of the engine at the points lever. The idea was that because the engine was low on steam it would continue past the points before the pressure in reverse stopped the engine and sent it back. I would just change the points and jump back onto the cab steps when the engine passed.

However, the steam pressure was extremely low and I began to panic because it looked as if the locomotive was not going to stop and it travelled ever nearer to the off-shed signal. It was a relief when the engine stopped just short of the signal. It began to move towards me, but it was quite a way from me and despite me hurrying towards it, it was picking up speed and when it passed I just managed to jump onto the step and grab the handle. I got into the cab, shut off the regulator and applied the brake but due to the lack of steam the brake had no effect.

I wound the gear forward again and opened the regulator, but that had no effect either. I rushed across and screwed on the tender hand brake. This had a little effect, but it was too late. The engine hit the three engines that were already standing on the back road, sending me across the footplate and causing an enormous bang that seemed to echo over the whole area. I ducked down and looked out through a join in the doors. The foreman had come out of his office and half a dozen men had come out of the cabin, my driver included. He walked down to the rails, looked into the engine shed, looked over to an engine by the turntable, and over to the engines on the back road. Everything looked all right. He scratched his head, turned and shrugged his shoulders towards the foreman and walked back to the cabin, assuming that the bang must have been caused by some shunting over in the goods yard.

I got off the far side of the engine and made my way to the concrete panelled fence on Middlewich Road. I climbed over and went to the corner shop (now CarBits), and bought myself a Broadhurst pie.

"Did you hear that big crash?" my driver said as I walked into the cabin.

"Never heard nothing," I said holding my pie up. "I must have been in the shop."

Over & Wharton

I moved out of the shed link, into the spare link and out onto the rails again. I was on the Over and Wharton shunt. We prepared our engine, 48151 and left Northwich light engine for the run to Winsford on the bottom line. Up the Arches, right at the branch to Wallerscote and Hartford Junction (LMS), then back along the bottom line tender first thundering through Hartford station and over the Weaver viaduct in the direction of Crewe. By Winsford signal box we crossed the line into the sidings and the small branch to Over and Wharton station. The goods yard had been kept open for local coalmen, but the station was closed long ago. Now though the goods yard was very busy.

I.C.I were using it to load rock salt. There was a massive wheeled tractor loading the wagons which were on either side of the mountain of salt. Once loaded it was our job to pull the loaded trains out to the sidings at Winsford junction and replace them with empties which had to be pushed down into the yard. The trains left Winsford for destinations all over the country. Northwich didn't get any work southbound, but we got quite a lot of work on the trains going north. It was not very busy on the shunt duty because it took quite a while to load the trucks, so a lot of time was spent in the office of the old station or, depending on the driver, across the road in The North Western Bar (now The Top House). All day long tipper lorries were running up Wharton hill from the salt works which were only ten minutes away down New Road. We did have a direct line to the works via the Winsford branch from Cuddington, but due to the amount of traffic, it was not possible to use it for the rock salt trains.

Midnight At Marbury

I was in The Ring O'Bells on the Old Warrington Road with Gordy and three local girls, who shall remain nameless. It was well after eleven o'clock and the landlord was trying to prise us from the place, but we were in no hurry to finish off our evening. We decided to head for Marbury – Gordy on his Honda with one of the girls, the other two squeezed up on the pillion of my James. We set off down the old I.C.I. road, arriving at Marbury we turned onto the track and rode up to the swimming pool. We hid the bikes behind some bushes, knowing that there were security patrols. The gates at the pool were not as formidable as they are now and it was an easy climb over, even for the girls.

It was midnight and we were lying on the grass, chatting, and exchanging fictitious tales about the ghost of the Marbury Lady. The ghost stories, the moonlit night, the shadowy trees and bushes, and the strange unexplained noises, made quite a scary scene. But if any of us were scared, we certainly would not let on to anyone else.

I walked across to the pool and reached down to the water. In the cool night air the water felt quite warm. I walked back to the gang.

"Shall we have a swim then?" I said. But none of them seemed very keen.

"Well, I'm going in," I said. I stripped down to my pants, and went back over to the pool, posing comically, showing of my slim, muscular, fireman's body for a few moments before diving into the water. Straight away I knew my pants had gone. I swam about the pool trying to find them, but in the darkness and with the ripples on the water every time I moved, it seemed like an impossible task.

"Lost your pants?" Gordy shouted smugly, causing laughter from the girls.

I swam to the edge and tried to coax the others to join me in the pool, but they weren't having it.

"Fetch my jeans over," I called.

One of the girls picked up my jeans, and then sat on them.

"Nah," she said. "You come and get them."

This could be a bit embarrassing I thought. I turned and looked in the pool, it had settled a bit but I could see nothing in the water. Luckily my embarrassment was saved by the security patrol. The only light was from the moon and stars so the glare from the patrolman's headlights could be seen well before he reached the pool gates. Gordy and the girls hid in the bushes and I rushed across, hastily dressing into my now wet clothes before joining them.

The security guard didn't open the gates, he just shone the torch around the pool before making a hasty departure. Perhaps he was a bit scared that the Marbury Lady would turn up.

Express Parcels

With the soda ash from Northwich and the salt from Winsford we were doing quite a lot of bottom line work, getting relief at Wigan, Preston, or Carnforth. On this occasion we were working from Winsford Junction with a train of rock salt for Perth. We had a Class 9, 92026. We left Winsford for a quick run up the fast line through Hartford and Acton Bridge to Weaver Junction. The driver Joe Mills was a passed fireman and he was having a great time, but by now I could handle anything so it caused me no problems. We passed through Warrington, Wigan, then arrived at Preston for relief. The driver contacted control and was told that they wanted us to work the Carlisle-Crewe express parcels through to Crewe. We had our break then walked across to the signal box to await our train. It was approaching the box some time after midnight and we made our way down to the trackside. The engine came into sight out of the misty darkness, hissing and puffing a little. The distinctive smoke deflectors made me think that it was Class 9, which surprised me because being a parcels train I was expecting a black five. Then I saw the three massive driving wheels. It was a big green Britannia, 70028. We left Preston and quickly picked up speed. We were soon travelling very fast indeed, it was terrific, we were like a couple of kids with a new toy, and every now and then one of us would get up and give a blast of the prairie whistle which was a novelty in itself. We got to Crewe non-stop, fast line all the way.

Stanlow

I was booked on with Ellis Richardson to relieve a train coming from the Middlewich branch. We relieved a lot here going to the steel works at Shotwick (Dee Marsh), or Ellesmere Port refineries. Often they were worked by Class 9's and when you reached the destination you usually had to take the engine to Birkenhead and travel home on the passenger service. We got on the engine, 92111 and set off on the line towards Chester. At Mouldsworth we collected our single line token from the signal box, then set off to the branch line on the right. It was downhill from here through tree lined cuttings and embankments with pleasant views across the plain to the Welsh hills.

Near the bottom we passed though the disused station at Helsby before joining double tracks again for the last leg to Stanlow. There was plenty going on at Stanlow with all the oil companies bunched together. It was a massive works and the smell of oil filled the air. We left the train of tanks in the sidings and set off for Birkenhead. *(The line from Mouldsworth to Helsby is now closed.)*

In the other direction, the Middlewich branch had always been busy, with empty coal/slack trucks from Shotwick or Northwich, and fuel tanks from Ellesmere Port (Stanlow). It was a nice run with no really hard gradients. It was a single track to Sandbach where the Stoke traffic would join the main line through Sandbach station before branching off on another single line through Wheelock to Kidsgrove. *(The line from Sandbach through Wheelock has been dismantled, but like so many other places the much older canal through the village is still in use.)* You'd carry on through the old Harecastle Tunnel at Kidsgrove and on into Stoke-on-Trent station, where you usually got relief. It was quite normal in those days to take your break over in the railway club, before reporting back to control for your return working.

The Silverdale empties used the same route until Sandbach, but then carried on down the main line through Crewe and on towards Stafford for about seven miles before turning right onto the branch line. There was no turning facility at the mine so the engine usually went tender first outward, returning engine first with the loaded trucks. On the branch line you'd have to run round the train and go engine first back over the top of the main line and on to the Silverdale Colliery near Newcastle-under-Lyme. After a break, and a visit to the well-equipped canteen, it was back tender-first with the loaded coal trucks to the main line junction, then engine-first back to Northwich. We'd travel quite fast on the slow line to Crewe, but we were frequently overtaken on the fast line by the Electric Flyers, who seemed at that time to be travelling at amazing speeds.

One of the firemen, Keith Elson was selling a motor bike, a BSA 350cc B31. There was nothing wrong with the James, but I thought I'd like a bigger bike so I bought it. It was totally different to the James. Not very fast, you'd struggle to do 70mph but it could tow a car. It had a monobloc carburettor fitted and a Gold Star silencer, but what I liked best was that the timing was slightly out. You could travel at 30mph then pull in the clutch, rev up the engine, and then completely shut off the throttle. A two foot flame would shoot out of the exhaust pipe accompanied by an enormous bang. I must admit I enjoyed frightening the daylights out of many an unwary pedestrian.

As I said before, drinking and riding motorcycles is not a good combination. One afternoon I was with Stan Sutton in The Ring O'Bells in Northwich. The other lads were at work, Stan was between jobs and I was on nightwork. We decided to go up to The Blue Cap in Sandiway for a game of bar billiards. Stan pestered me to drive so I let him loose on the BSA and I rode pillion. We absolutely flew through Castle, Greenbank and Hartford. "Slow down," I shouted as we approached the bend before the bridge over the dual carriageway. My words had no effect. That's it, I thought, hospital cases, there's no way this heavy old bike could take the corner at the speed we were doing. Luckily Stan realised and as there was nothing coming the other way he shot across the road and down the hill. I was relieved but the ordeal was not over. We carried on down slowed down at the bottom, but then pulled away across the road over the grass and onto the other carriageway before accelerating off towards The Blue Cap. Stan was in hysterics when we got there, and Stan being Stan I had to join in the laughter, but I was not really impressed.

We had a drink and a few games of bar billiards then set off back to Northwich. Stan hinted about driving back, but I made sure I got to the bike first. We had a drink in The Crown then decided to set off for the last drink in The Ark at Winsford. We had just passed The Volunteer and I performed the old exhaust explosion on two young girls that were on the pavement. As our laughter died down towards the arches we noticed a car had run into the back of another outside the old Co-Op building. Two elderly men were arguing and it looked like they were about to come to blows. We laughed as we

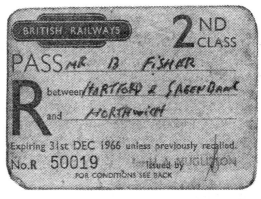

My pass for a safer mode of transport!

looked back at them. I looked forward again just as we hit the kerb under the arch. Stan finished up lying on the pavement and I was lying in the road with the bike on top of me.

The faulty ignition timing, as well as allowing the exhaust rick, also caused the front of the exhaust to become very hot and it would glow a purple/blue colour. That was the bit that was resting on my leg. I couldn't move the bike but Stan came over and pulled it off me, still laughing of course, but I was not in the mood for laughing with the great golf ball sized blister on my leg. We changed our mind about The Ark and decided to call across to The Bowling Green instead.

Shed Again

Late 1967, there was a lot of dieselisation going on and many of the jobs that we were relieving were turning up with diesels on the front. There was also a decline in the condition of the steamers. It was quite common to get on an engine with water leaking from the tubes or steam escaping from the pistons. Once the defects got too bad the engine was just withdrawn from service and replaced with one from a recently dieselised depot. We had lost our Class 2 pilot engine which had been replaced by a diesel shunter.

We had lost some of our work due to dieselisation and I was put back into the shed link. It was a bit different on shed now with the amount of diesels about you didn't get the same build-up of jobs to be done, so it was taking longer for the driver to fill his ticket. We still got away early but nowhere near as much as before. The steamers were coming on shed now in a terrible state. We disposed of our engines properly, but we rarely bothered to open the smoke boxes of 'foreign' engines. Other sheds seemed to be doing the same because when our own engines came back from other depots the smoke boxes were often full to the blast ring.

Dieselisation

The end of February 1968, was the week of dieselisation at Northwich. It happened pretty quickly once it started. As the diesels arrived the steamers that they replaced had their motions (side connecting rods) removed and were lined up on the back road of the shed, awaiting disposal. In my opinion the drivers generally accepted the change as progress, as if it were an improvement in their status. The firemen were not so happy, wondering if they had a future at the shed.

The shedmen were reduced from two crews per shift to one, so at the end of the week I moved back up into the now extended spare link.

I had been in the spare link over a month and it had been all diesel work. I hadn't been given a job and was sitting in the rest room playing cards with some of the other lads. The foreman walked in and asked Eddie Atherton to relieve a Runcorn train that was approaching the station.

"Take him with you," he said, and pointed to me. "It's a steamer, do you think he can still manage it?"

"If he can't, then nobody can," came the reply. This was quite a compliment and made me feel terrific and perhaps a little embarrassed, but not for long as I was up like a shot and eager to go.

We arrived on the footplate, it was a Class 8, 48168, and we set off for Runcorn. We were in no rush – the driver opened up a little from Hartford Junction to Weaver Junction – but other han that we just chugged along. We both knew that this would be our very last trip on a steam engine and we wanted to enjoy every minute.

Fun at Pickmere

There was a gang of us in the Roebuck one Saturday afternoon. Me, Gordy, Stan Sutton, Tommy Walsh, Jimmy Co and a few others. It was closing time. Rudheath Club for a few games of snooker was the usual option, but we decided to go to The Jubilee Club for a change. A car and two motorcycles descended on Pickmere, but the club was closed. We made our way down to the lake. The small funfair was of no interest to us, but the rowing boats, that could be a laugh. We had a boat each and it was not long before one of us got splashed. We were all up then, hitting the oars into the water aiming at each other, wobbling all the time and trying to keep balance in the boats. Trying to position ourselves on the outside because you would get drenched if caught in a crossfire.

We were all soaked, all except Jimmy that is, who kept well out of the way. He was no fool and realised what was about to happen when we all began to row towards him. He tried to make it to the bank and probably would have done if Stan hadn't leapt into the water. Fortunately the water was not that deep, just below his waist. He dashed across and jumped on the side of Jimmy's boat, tipping the boat up and sending Jimmy into the lake.

We left the boatman to gather up the rowing boats. He was not over pleased and shouted that we were all banned from the lake. But we'd had a laugh, and the small crowd watching us from the lakeside seemed to have enjoyed the show as well.

Scrap

There was a line of dead steam engines on the back road of the shed. They had all had their side rods removed, ready to be towed away for scrap. A Type 2 diesel was booked to take three of them to Crewe, 48151, 48639, and 48421. I was put on the one

Preserved ex-Northwich Stanier Class 8, No. 48151, seen heading an enthusiast special. Photo: John Shuttleworth. Courtesy: West Coast Railway Co. Ltd.

at the rear to act as brakeman. The engines had started to rust and had been attacked by souvenir hunters. I had fired these engines many times and it was sad to see these once powerful machines in such a state. We set off for Crewe down the Middlewich branch line. It was strange to be sitting on a dead engine, my mind wandering back to happier working days. Fortunately, 48151 never reached the scrap furnaces, it was bought for preservation (see photograph overleaf).

Two weeks later I was booked on as brakeman again. Three more engines: 48632, 48036, 48272. We were to take them to the siding at a place called Tibshelf in Derbyshire. These were the last steam engines to leave Northwich.

Last Days

I was on Wallerscote tripper with Ernie Weaver with a Type 4 diesel. We were just approaching Hartford Junction (C.L.C.) when I burst into song like I often did.

"Yummy, yummy, yummy, I got love in my tummy," was as far as I got.

Ernie burst into hysterics.

"Yummy, yummy, yummy! Bloody hell! *Yummy, yummy yummy!"* followed by laughter.

That's all I got for the rest of the day. I always found Ernie to be a funny man. I liked working with people like Ernie during the diesel days. The light-hearted humour gave a bit of relief from the repetitive boredom of second man duties.

I knew that I would eventually be offered redundancy money, but I couldn't stand the boredom any longer (see chart of comparative duties, overleaf) and decided to go ahead and join the Royal Air Force. I worked my last second man duty with Ernie Southern. We had a small diesel shunter working a ballast train for the P. Way gang at Greenbank. The next day I would be off to R.A.F. Swinderby in Lincolnshire, to start my recruit training.

Comparison between the two different types of traction on a typical trip:

Book on duty. Read notices. Enquire for particulars of job driver and engine.

——————————— Proceed to engine. ———————————

Stanier Class 8	Type 2 Diesel
Check water level in boiler. Test gauge cocks and check pressure. Start to prepare the fire and take any action required to raise steam or boiler water level if necessary.	
Go to stores for tools: firing shovel, pick, lamps and bucket containing detonators and spanners.	
Check fire irons are in recess in tender: dart and paddle (long-handled shovel for removing fire in an emergency).	
Check the coal is safely stacked on the tender.	
Check tender water level gauge and do a visual check inside the tender in case the level gauge is faulty.	
Check that the smoke box has been emptied of ash and the door is securely closed.	
Fill sand boxes.	Fill sand boxes, collect detonators. Check lights/lamps.
When engine is prepared raise pressure and test both water injectors.	
Make a brew in the billycan.	Make a brew in billycan.

——————————— On leaving the sidings ———————————

Maintain efficient firebed. Maintain steam pressure and ensure the water in the boiler is kept at a safe level by use of exhaust or live steam injector. Regulate air supply via dampers and firedoors to obtain maximum combustion efficiency.	In theory it could be said that firemen were route learning, but most firemen knew the routes quite well already. Looking out of the window at the scenery was quite pleasant for a while but it soon became repetitive and tedious.
Prepare coal by breaking lumps with the coal pick. Keep the cab floor as clean as is practically possible. Keep a look out on the driver's blind side for signals and obstructions.	

When stopped at a signal go to signalbox or if a phone is at the signal use
telephone to contact signalman at intervals.

———————————— On return to depot ————————————

Stanier Class 8	Type 2 Diesel
Run down fire prior to going on shed while still maintaining sufficient steam pressure to keep the boiler safe and work the engine controls.	
Carry out disposal of the fire if required by the shed foreman.	
Return tools to stores	Return any tools to stores
Book off.	Book off.

STEAM DUTIES

All non firing days, rest days, bank holidays, annual holidays, sick days, and spare duties without a driver, have been omitted.

Diesel turns are in italics.

DATE	DAY	JOB	DRIVER	LOCOMOTIVE
28.06.65	M	Oakleigh Tripper	Dennis Lewis	48640
03.07.65	Sa	Light Engine Edge Hill	Harry Naylor	77014
05.07.65	M	Wallerscote Tripper	Don France	48639
06.07.65	Tu	Shed	Eric Falland	
08.07.65	Th	Wallerscote Tripper	Don France	48639
09.07.65	F	Shed	Joe Fisher	
12.07.65	M	Winsford Pilot	Bill Elson	46487
13.07.65	Tu	Ballast Train (P Way)	Len Higgins	77011
14.07.65	W	Wallerscote Tripper	Ernie Southern	48315
17.07.65	Sa	Oakleigh Tripper	Danny Norrie	48135
20.07.65	Tu	Shed	Jack Jones	
22.07.65	Th	Oakleigh Tripper	Ernie Southern	48374
23.07.65	F	Wallerscote Tripper	Frank Sissons	48639
24.07.65	Sa	Oakleigh Tripper	Ernie Southern	48315
26.07.65	M	Oakleigh Tripper	Jimmy Riley	48631
27.07.65	Tu	Ballast	Jack Newton	48374
31.07.65	Sa	Shed	Jack Nicolson	
06.08.65	F	Shed	Jack Nicolson	
09.08.65	M	Wallerscote Tripper	Don France	48135
10.08.65	Tu	Oakleigh Tripper	Vic Johnson	48135
11.08.65	W	Winsford Pilot	Joe Stretch	46487
Turns 22-26		Shed	Joe Fisher(2) Johnny Adamson(1)	
			Roy Holland(1) Eric Birkenhead(1)	
02.09.65	*Th*	*Trafford Park*	*Doug Sunderland*	
04.09.65	Sa	Heaton Mersey (Cancelled)	Joe Walker	
06.09.65	M	Wallerscote Tripper	Ron Bowden	48462
07.09.65	Tu	Marston Pilot	Alf Ward	46487
08.09.65	W	Wallerscote Tripper	Eddie Atherton	48640
11.09.65	Sa	Pilot	Harry Naylor	46487
12.09.65	Su	Shed	Alf Beech	
14.09.65	Tu	Oakleigh Tripper	Jim Naylor	48374
15.09.65	W	Oakleigh Tripper	Jim Naylor	48118
16.09.65	Th	Wallerscote Tripper	Ernie Southern	48639
17.09.65	F	Oakleigh Tripper	Jim Naylor	48155
18.09.65	Sa	Oakleigh Tripper	Jim Naylor	48305
23.09.65	Th	Godley (1st main line turn)	Ernie Southern	48528
29.09.65	W	Clockface	Joe Fisher	48615
04.10.65	M	Wallerscote Tripper	Ernie Southern	48631

14.10.65	Th	Dee Marsh	Eddie Atherton	48155
15.10.65	*F*	*Hoppers Peak Forest*	*Charlie Flecture/Jim Bate*	*D????*
19.10.65	Tu	Wallerscote Tripper	Ernie Weaver	48500
20.10.65	W	Pickup	Doug Sunderland	48500
21.10.65	Th	Light Engine Garston	Johnny Peters	90395
23.10.65	Sa	Glazebrook	Trafford Park driver	48327
29.10.65	F	Stoke	Charlie Flecture	45093
30.10.65	*Sa*	*Ballast Train*	*Joe Fisher*	*D3870(Shunter)*
01.11.65	M	Wallerscote Tripper	Don France	48395
05.11.65	F	Godley (Passed for main line)	Doug Sunderland	92053
06.11.65	Sa	Wallerscote Tripper	Don France	48155
08.11.65	M	Oakleigh Tripper	Ernie Weaver	48155
09.11.65	Tu	Shed	Roy Holland	
10.11.65	W	Shotwick/Ellesmere Port	Johnny Peters	92046
11.11.65	Th	Oakleigh Tripper	Ernie Weaver	48155
12.11.65	F	Light to Hartford Junction	Johnny Peters	48310
14.11.65	Su	Ballast Train	Jimmy Jones	48683
15.11.65	M	Light Engine Dallam	Johnny Adamson	48411
20.11.65	Sa	Dee Marsh	Don France	48408
22.11.65	*M*	*Halewood*	*Don Farrow*	*D5278*
24.11.65	W	Dee Marsh	George Blease	48735
26.11.65	F	Shed	Norman Adams	
29.11.65	M	Winsford Pilot	Don France/Alf Ward	46487
01.12.65	W	Saltney	Harry Greenwood	48631
02.12.65	Th	Winsford Pilot	Joe Stretch	46487
04.12.65	Sa	Barnsley Tanks	Jack Newton	45284
06.12.65	M	Passenger Chester Northgate	Frank Sissons	45393
07.12.65	Tu	Passenger Chester Northgate	Frank Sissons	45187
08.12.65	W	Wallerscote Tripper	Jim Naylor	48118
09.12.65	Th	Wallerscote Tripper	Jim Naylor	48118
10.12.65	F	Stoke Tanks	Eddie Atherton	48548 92029
11.12.65	Sa	Stoke Tanks	Johnny Adamson	92163
12.12.65	*Su*	*Trafford Park*	*Enoch Carter*	*D5275*
13.12.65	M	Healey Mills	Doug Sunderland	90329
14.12.65	Tu	Hoppers Peak Forest	Eddie Atherton	92029
15.12.65	W	Glazebrook	Trafford Park Driver	48690
16.12.65	Th	Relieve Hoppers	Johnny Adamson	92021
18.12.65	Sa	Healey Mills	Roy Holland	48118
20.12.65	M	Dee Marsh	Vic Johnson	48701
21.12.65	Tu	Warrington	George Blease	48057
22.12.65	*W*	*Halewood*	*Joe Walker*	*D5275*
23.12.65	Th	Godley	Eric Falland	48421
29.12.65	W	Saint Helens	Eric Falland	92126

STEAM DUTIES

Date	Day	Duty	Driver	Loco
30.12.65	Th	Wallerscote Tripper	Jack Newton	48631
04.01.66	Tu	Oakleigh Tripper	Ernie Southern	48118
05.01.66	W	Woolie Colliery	Jack Jones	48731
07.01.66	F	Oakleigh Tripper	Ernie Southern	48717
08.01.66	Sa	Oakleigh Tripper	Frank Darlington	48398
10.01.66	M	Healey Mills	Carl Bate	92024
11.01.66	Tu	Winsford Sidings	Len Higgins	44688
12.01.66	W	Partington	Johnny Adamson	48057
14.01.66	F	Winsford Sidings	Len Higgins	77011
15.01.66	Sa	Winsford Sidings	Eric Gregory	77011
16.01.66	Su	Oakleigh Tripper	Jack Spencer	48476
17.01.66	M	Dee Marsh	Clary Egerton	48670
18.01.66	Tu	Godley Cancelled (sidings)	Eddie Brown	48176
19.01.66	W	Stoke	Jack Cross	45376
20.01.66	Th	Stoke	Jack Cross	48200
21.01.66	F	Stoke	Jack Cross	92023
22.01.65	Sa	Shed	Eddie Atherton	
24.01.66	M	Shed	Jack Chadwick	
25.01.66	Tu	Wallerscote Tripper	Johnny Adamson	48717
26.01.66	W	Saltney	Ernie Weaver	48398
27.01.66	Th	Northwich triangle/Turning engines	Ernie Weaver	(Turntable broken)
28.01.66	F	Shotwick	Roy Holland	92133
29.01.66	Sa	Glazebrook	Trafford Park Driver	48652
31.01.66	M	Dee Marsh	Jim Bate	48717
01.02.66	Tu	Partington	Jim Bate	48239
02.02.66	W	Wallerscote Tripper	Ernie Weaver	48155
03.02.66	Th	Shotwick	Frank Sissons	48118
04.02.66	F	Dee Marsh	Frank Sissons	48118
05.02.66	Sa	Wallerscote Tripper	Ernie Weaver	48155
06.02.66	Su	Sunday Tripper	Joe Tomkinson	48155
08.02.66	Tu	Ballast Train	Johnny Peters	92092
10.02.66	Th	Saint Helens	Eric Falland	45330
11.02.66	F	Saint Helens	Carl Bate	45275
12.02.66	Sa	Winsford Sidings	Ken Walker	48735
13.02.66	Su	Godley	Ernie Southern	48201
14.02.66	M	Runcorn	Jack Jones	45???
15.02.66	Tu	Godley	Harry Greenwood	92166
16.02.66	W	Shed	Eddie Atherton	
17.02.66	Th	Clockface	Don France	48462
22.02.66	Tu	Dee Marsh	Eddie Atherton	48118
23.02.66	W	Dee Marsh	Eddie Atherton	48639
24.02.66	Th	Dee Marsh	Eddie Atherton	48639
25.02.66	F	Dee Marsh	Eddie Atherton	48631

Date	Day	Location	Name	Number
26.02.66	Sa	Dee Marsh	Ron Carey	48640
28.02.66	M	Wallerscote Tripper	Alan Webb	48017
01.03.66	Tu	Wallerscote Tripper	Alan Webb	48639
02.03.66	W	Shawfield	Frank Sissons	44987
03.03.66	Th	Wallerscote Tripper	Alan Webb	48631
04.03.66	F	Wallerscote Tripper	Alan Webb	48640
05.03.66	Sa	Runcorn	Alan Webb	48692
07.03.66	M	Shed	Johnny Adamson	
09.03.66	W	Partington	Ken Bate	92085
10.03.66	Th	Saltney	Joe Walker	48735
11.03.66	F	Saltney	Ken Walker	48118
12.03.66	Sa	Hoppers Peak Forest	George Blease	48073
14.03.66	M	Dee Marsh	Bill Stringer	48100
15.03.66	Tu	Godley	Ernie Weaver	92070
16.03.66	W	Godley	Joe Walker	92070
17.03.66	Th	Stoke	Johnny Woodier	92106
18.03.66	F	Stoke	Fred Newton	92107
19.03.66	Sa	Spare	George Blease	
21.03.66	M	Dee Marsh	Vic Johnson	48643
22.03.66	Tu	Dee Marsh	Fred Newton	48643
23.03.66	W	Dee Marsh	Fred Newton	48717
24.03.66	Th	Ellesmere Port	George Blease	92045
25.03.66	F	Barnsley Tanks	Eric Birkenhead	48268
28.03.66	M	Wallerscote Tripper	Vic Johnson	48408
29.03.66	Tu	Wallerscote Tripper	Vic Johnson	48640
30.03.66	W	Stoke	George Blease	48687
31.03.66	Th	Wallerscote Tripper	Vic Johnson	48717
01.04.66	F	Wallerscote Tripper	Jim Bell	48640
05.04.66	Tu	Ribble	Jack Cross	92056
06.04.66	W	Spare	Jim Bate	
07.04.66	Th	Oakleigh Tripper	Ernie Weaver	48057
09.04.66	Sa	Partington	Frank Sissons	48766
12.04.66	Tu	Dee Marsh Cancelled(Spare)	Frank Sissons	
13.04.66	W	Stoke	Fred Newton	48662
14.04.66	Th	Stoke	Fred Newton	92046
15.04.66	F	Stoke	Fred Newton	92032
18.04.66	M	Ash Bridge	Eric Gregory	48408
19.04.66	Tu	Glazebrook	Trafford Park Driver	48344
20.04.66	W	Dewsnap	Jack Cross	48631
21.04.66	Th	Runcorn	Jack Jones	92070
22.04.66	F	Shotwick	Fred Newton	48738
23.04.66	Sa	Gowhole	Jack Cross	48639
25.04.66	M	Oakleigh Tripper	Don France	48631

STEAM DUTIES

26.04.66	Tu	Shed	Brian Taylor	
28.04.66	Th	Oakleigh Tripper	Don France	48631
29.04.66	F	Oakleigh Tripper	Jack Newton	48639
30.04.66	Sa	Oakleigh Tripper	Don France	48643
02.05.66	M	Godley, Cancelled Plumley	Charlie Coppack	92083
05.05.66	Th	Dee Marsh	Roy Holland	48639
06.05.66	F	Ellesmere Port	Jack Jones	48642
07.05.55	Sa	Healey Mills	Jack Cross	48301
09.05.66	M	Corkickal	Johnny Peters	48683
10.05.66	Tu	Corkickal	Johnny Peters	48717
11.05.66	W	Corkickal	Johnny Peters	48100
12.05.66	Th	Corkickal	Johnny Peters	48176
13.05.66	F	Cheadle	Henry Lloyd	48256
15.05.66	Su	Shed	Hector Dodd	
17.05.66	Tu	Dee Marsh	Ron Bowden	48363
18.05.66	W	Dee Marsh	Ron Bowden	48464
20.05.66	F	Dee Marsh	Ron Bowden	48717
21.05.66	Sa	Dee Marsh	Ken Bate	48683
23.05.66	M	Dee Marsh	Roy Holland	42782
24.05.66	Tu	Pickup	Roy Holland	46405
25.05.66	W	Partington	Hector Dodd	92026
26.05.66	Th	Ellesmere Port	Sid Clarke	44685
Turns	197-201	Shed	Roy Holland(1) Fred Corker(4)	
04.06.66	Sa	Godley	Joe Mills	48462
Turns	203-207	Shed	Wilf Egerton(5)	
13.06.66	M	Godley	Ron Bowden	48324
14.06.66	Tu	Dee Marsh	Joe Walker	48683
15.06.66	W	Godley	Hector Dodd	45131
16.06.66	Th	Trafford Park	George Blease	48???
17.06.66	F	Godley	Hector Dodd	92082
18.06.66	Sa	Dee Marsh	Hector Dodd	48100
19.06.66	*Su*	*Trafford Park*	*Eric Falland*	*D5278*
20.06.66	M	Graded as Fireman, started in the shed link with Jack Nicolson.		
Turns	216-220	Shed	Jack Nicolson(5)	
25.06.66	Sa	Oakleigh Tripper	Roy Holland	48683
Turns	232-267	Shed	Jack Nicolson(10) Frank Sissons(5) Joe Mills(3) Fred Corker(1) Chris Hughes(1) Roy Holland (5), Johnny Adamson(4) Len Higgins(5)	
25.08.66	Th	Ash Bridge	Albert Tilley	48683
26.08.66	F	Shed	Joe Mills	
30.08.66	Tu	Out of Shed Link and into the Spare Link.		
		Wallerscote Tripper	Johnny Woodier	48640

.08.66	W	Wallerscote Tripper	Johnny Woodier	48640
.09.66	Th	Glazebrook	Joe Walker	48155
2.09.66	F	Wallerscote Tripper	Johnny Woodier	48693
5.09.66	M	Lght Engine Dallam	Keith Jackson	48???
4.09.66	W	Dee Marsh	Alf Beech	48643
5.09.66	Th	Godley	Keith Jackson	92083
5.09.66	F	Dewsnap	Jim Naylor	48377
7.09.66	Sa	Dewsnap	Jim Naylor	48693
3.09.66	Su	Ballast Train	Charlie Cooper	48631
.09.66	M	Ravenhead	Johnny Woodier	92233
.09.66	Tu	Ravenhead	Johnny Woodier	48462
.09.66	W	Ravenhead	Johnny Woodier	48408
2.09.66	Th	Ravenhead	Johnny Woodier	48272
3.09.66	F	Ravenhead	Johnny Woodier	48334
5.09.66	M	Over & Wharton Shunt	Frank Sissons	48151 (Saved)
7.09.66	Tu	Over & Wharton Shunt	Frank Sissons	48151 (Saved)
3.09.66	W	Over & Wharton Shunt	Frank Sissons	48151 (Saved)
.09.66	F	Over & Wharton Shunt	Frank Sissons	48151 (Saved)
5.10.66	Th	Oakleigh Tripper	Alf Beech	48334
7.10.66	F	Wallerscote Tripper	Ken Walford	48462
3.10.66	Sa	Carlisle	Bill Stringer	48100
.10.66	M	Over & Wharton Shunt	Tony Longdon	48151 (Saved)
.10.66	Tu	Spare	Herbert Ratcliffe	
2.10.66	W	Over & Wharton Shunt	Ellis Richardson	48151 (Saved)
3.10.66	Th	Light Engine Sutton Oak	Eddie Brown	48149
4.10.66	F	Whitehaven	Danny Norrie	92231
ırns	299-302	Shed	Herbert Ratcliffe(1) David May(3)	
.10.66	Th	Godley	Ken Walford	92160
.10.66	F	Shed	David May	
4.10.66	M	Wallerscote Tripper	Ron Curzon	48100
5.10.66	Tu	Oakleigh Tripper	Johnny Woodier	48699
5.10.66	W	Silverdale	Ernie Southern	48???
7.10.66	Th	Runcorn	Alan Fulton	48752
ırns	309-313	Shed	Brian Taylor(5)	
3.11.66	Tu	Dee Marsh	Ken Walford	48305
9.11.66	W	Dee Marsh	Ken Walford	48640
0.11.66	Th	Dee Marsh	Ken Walford	48271
.11.66	F	Dee Marsh	Ken Walford	48717
4.11.66	M	Shed	David May	
5.11.66	Tu	Shotwick	David May	48272
ırns	320-327	Shed	David May(6) Fred Corker(1) Chris Hughes(1)	
5.11.66	F	Ellesmere Port	Eric Walker	92046

26.11.66	Sa	Shed	David May	
28.11.66	M	Wallerscote Tripper	Ellis Richardson	48693
29.11.66	Tu	Wallerscote Tripper	Ellis Richardson	48272
30.11.66	W	Spare	Ellis Richardson	
01.12.66	Th	Wallerscote Tripper	Ellis Richardson	48681
02.12.66	F	Wallerscote Tripper	Jim Riley	48334
05.12.66	M	Godley	Ken Walford	92096
06.12.66	Tu	Wallerscote Tripper	Ken Walford	48681
07.12.66	W	Shotwick	Bill Elson	48100
08.12.66	Th	Oakleigh Tripper	Ken Walford	48640
09.12.66	F	Ellesmere Port	Ken Walford	48110
10.12.66	Sa	Guide Bridge	Tony Longdon	90265
12.12.66	M	Dee Marsh	Jack Newton	48334
13.12.66	Tu	Ravenhead	Ken Walford	48631
14.12.66	W	Ravenhead	Ken Walford	48151 (Saved)
15.12.66	Th	Ravenhead	Ken Walford	48304
16.12.66	F	Ravenhead	Ken Walford	48631
18.12.66	Su	Ballast Train	Sam Rowlands	48640
19.12.66	M	Shed	Ken Walford	
20.12.66	Tu	Godley	Eric Gregory	75037
21.12.66	W	Godley	Eric Gregory	48735
22.12.66	Th	Godley	Eric Gregory	48410
23.12.66	F	Godley	Eric Gregory	48336
Turns	349-351	Shed	Fred Corker(3)	
31.12.66	Sa	Warrington	Ken Walford	48057
02.01.67	M	Ellesmere Port	Ellis Richardson	92111
Turns	354-359	Shed	Fred Corker(5) Ken Bate(1)	
10.01.67	Tu	Godley	Henry Lloyd	44863
11.01.67	W	Godley	Henry Lloyd	45232
12.01.67	Th	Godley	Henry Lloyd	48057
13.01.67	F	Pickup	Charlie Wright	46440
14.01.67	Sa	Over & Wharton Shunt	Henry Lloyd	48153
Turns	365-368	Shed	Wilf Egerton(4)	
20.01.67	F	Oakleigh Tripper	Ken Walford	48643
21.01.67	Sa	Shed	Wilf Egerton	
23.01.67	M	Shed	Brian Taylor	
24.01.67	Tu	Dee Marsh	Charlie Cooper	48272
25.01.67	W	Shed	Brian Taylor	
26.01.67	Th	Dee Marsh	Joe Mills	48640
27.01.67	F	Dee Marsh	Albert Tilley	48683
28.01.67	Sa	Dee Marsh	Albert Tilley	48717
Turns	377-383	Shed	Brian Taylor(s) Charlie Coppack(1) Chris Hughes(1)	

12.06.67	M	Wallerscote Tripper	George Coppack	48212
13.06.67	Tu	Wallerscote Tripper	George Coppack	48650
14.06.67	W	Wallerscote Tripper	George Coppack	48650
15.06.67	Th	Wallerscote Tripper	Jack Jones	48650
16.06.67	F	Wallerscote Tripper	George Coppack	48639
17.06.67	Sa	Wallerscote Tripper	George Coppack	48033
19.06.67	M	Warrington	Henry Lloyd	48408
20.06.67	Tu	Warrington	Henry Lloyd	48722
21.06.67	W	Larbert	Henry Lloyd	70049(Britannia)
22.06.67	Th	Warrington	Henry Lloyd	48304
10.07.67	*M*	*Pickup*	*Chris Hughes/Ellis Richardson*	*D12017(Sh)*
11.07.67	Tu	Parcels	Don Farrow	48151 (Saved)
12.07.67	W	Spare	Johnny Peter	
13.07.67	Th	Shed	Fred Corker	
15.07.67	Sa	Shed	Fred Corker	
17.07.67	M	Shotwick	Fred Newton	92131
18.07.67	Tu	Shotwick	Fred Newton	48085
19.07.67	W	Shotwick	Fred Newton	48119
20.07.67	Th	Shotwick	Fred Newton	92024
21.07.67	F	Light Engine Dallam	Fred Newton	48683
24.07.67	M	Dee Marsh	Frank Darlington	48271
25.07.67	Tu	Dee Marsh/Ellesmere Port	Clary Egerton	48212
26.07.67	W	Dee Marsh	Ken Walker	48639
27.07.67	Th	Winsford-Carlisle	Johnny Peters	48033
29.07.67	Sa	Dewsnap	Jack Cross	48683
31.07.67	M	Spare	Ken Bate	
01.08.67	Tu	Warrington	Jack Cross	48750
02.08.67	W	Warrington	Ken Bate	48271
03.08.67	Th	Warrington	Jack Cross	48727
04.08.67	F	Corkickal	Henry Lloyd	48639
Turns	519-523	Shed	Joe Mills(5)	
17.08.67	Th	Pilot	Wilf Moss	48421
20.08.67	Su	Shed	Wilf Egerton	
21.08.67	*M*	*Light Engine From Crewe*	*Frank Darlington*	*D7674*
22.08.67	*Tu*	*Trafford Park*	*David May*	*D5278*
23.08.67	*W*	*Trafford Park*	*David May*	*D5278/D5276*
24.08.67	*Th*	*Trafford Park*	*David May*	*D 7586/D5276*
25.08.67	*F*	*Larbert*	*Harry Naylor*	*D 7674*
29.08.67	*Tu*	*Shed*	*Clary Egerton*	
30.08.67	W	*Shotwick* L/Engine Birkenhead	Sam Gandy	D289 92234
31.08.67	Th	Middlesborough	Jack Spencer	48735
1.09.67	F	Warrington-Willesden	Frank Darlington	43021
2.09.67	*Sa*	*L/Engine Warrington Crewe*	*Jim Bate*	*D5026 D7672*

STEAM DUTIES

04.09.67	M	Edge Hill	Jeff Cookson	48735
05.09.67	Tu	Shed	Wilf Egerton	
06.09.67	W	Saint Helens	Eddie Brown	44864
07.09.67	Th	Saint Helens	Eddie Brown	*45???*
11.09.67	*M*	*Stoke*	*Charlie Wright*	*D5197/7585 D342*
14.09.67	*Th*	*Hoppers Peak Forest*	*Joe Walker*	*D7585**
15.09.67	*F*	*Hoppers Peak Forest*	*Joe Walker*	*D7275**
16.09.67	*Sa*	*Hoppers Peak Forest*	*Sam Gandy*	*D5277**
19.09.67	Tu	Larbert	Johnny Peters	48033
20.09.67	*W*	*Hoppers Peak Forest*	*Harry Langston*	*D5279**
21.09.67	*Th*	*Hoppers Peak Forest*	*Joe Greenwood*	*D7586**
22.09.67	*F*	*Hoppers Peak Forest*	*Joe Greenwood*	*D5276**
23.09.67	Sa	Spare	Harry Langston	
25.09.67	M	Spare	Ken Walker	
26.09.67	Tu	Ravenhead	Hector Dodd	48683
27.09.67	W	Ravenhead	Hector Dodd	48033
28.09.67	Th	Ravenhead	Hector Dodd	48639
29.09.67	F	Ravenhead	Hector Dodd	48033
02.10.67	*Mo*	*Hoppers Peak Forest*	*Henry Lloyd*	*D7586**
03.10.67	*Tu*	*Hoppers Peak Forest*	*Charlie Cooper*	*D5279**
05.10.67	*Th*	*Hoppers Peak Forest*	*Jim Bate*	*D7586**
06.10.67	*F*	*Hoppers Peak Forest*	*Jim Bate*	*D5279**
07.10.67	Sa	Whitehaven	David May	48340
08.10.67	Su	Over & Wharton Shunt	John Yarwood	48631
09.10.67	M	Runcorn	Jack Newton	48329
10.10.67	Tu	Dee Marsh	Jack Newton	48033
11.10.67	W	Dee Marsh	Jack Newton	48151(Saved)
12.10.67	Th	Dee Marsh	Jack Newton	48746
13.10.67	F	Dee Marsh	Jack Newton	48036
18.10.67	W	Tow Failed Diesel to Trafford Park	Harry Langston	44658
19.10.67	*Th*	*Pilot*	*Eric Birkenhead*	*D3109(Shunter)*
20.10.67	F	Silverdale	Alan Coppack	48722
21.10.67	Sa	Ballast Train	Ken Walker	48036
23.10.67	*M*	*Stoke*	*Doug Sunderland*	*D7600 D3??*
24.10.67	*Tu*	*Stoke*	*Doug Sunderland*	*D291 D332*
25.10.67	*W*	*Stoke*	*Doug Sunderland*	*D7524/D7516 D327*
30.10.67	*M*	*Silverdale*	*Henry Lloyd*	*D 7551*
31.10.67	Tu	Silverdale	Henry Lloyd	48639
01.11.67	W	Silverdale	Ron Carey	48151(Saved)
02.11.67	Th	Silverdale	Ron Carey	48727
04.11.67	Sa	Runcorn	Ron Carey	45114

Union dispute requires second man on hopper

BRUCE FISHER

Turns	581-585	Shed	Fred Corker(5)	
13.11.67	M	Wallerscote Tripper	Gerald Coppack	48639
Turns	587-589	Shed	Fred Corker(3)	
18.11.67	*Sa*	*Pilot*	*George Blease*	*D3546(Shunter)*
19.11.67	*Su*	*Ballast Train*	*Frank Darlington*	*D3353 (Shunter)*
Turns	592-620	Shed	Fred Corker(29) Eddie Brown(1)	
31.12.67	*Su*	*Ballast Trains*	*Eric Gregory D3399(Sh) D5291 D7557*	
01.01.68	M	Over & Wharton Shunt	Carl Bate	48723
Turns	623-632	Shed	Fred Corker(10)	
15.01.68	*M*	*Warrington*	*Joe Greenwood*	*D5275*
16.01.68	Tu	Corkickal	Joe Greenwood	48632
17.01.68	W	Corkickal	Joe Greenwood	48063
19.01.68	*F*	*Warrington*	*Joe Greenwood*	*D5279*
Turns	637-651	Shed	Fred Corker(14) Jack Newton(1)	
12.02.68	M	Edge Hill	Vic Johnson	48722
13.02.68	Tu	Spare	Vic Johnson	
14.02.68	W	Wallerscote Tripper	Ken Walford	48036
15.02.68	Th	Wallerscote Tripper	Vic Johnson	48036
16.02.68	F	Wallerscote Tripper	Vic Johnson	48493
18.02.68	Su	Pilotman's Engine	Joe Fisher	48493(am)
				D7547(pm)
Turns	660-668	Shed	Fred Corker(8) Eric Gregory(1)	
04.03.68	W	*Into extended spare (Diesel) link*		
		Turns 669-683 All Diesel Work (Second Man)		
27.03.68	W	Runcorn (last steam turn)	Eddie Atherton	48168
		Turns 685-717 All Diesel Work		
14.05.68	Tu	Travel as brakeman to Crewe with 48151, 48639, 48421.		
		Turns 719-727 All Diesel Work		
28.05.68	Tu	Brakeman to Tibshelf with 48632, 48036, 48272. Last engines to		
		leave.		
		Turns 729-811 All Diesel work		
15.09.68	*Su*	*811 Last BR duty Ballast train*	*E Southern*	*D3354 (Shunter)*

Léonie Press local books include:

MEMORIES OF A CHESHIRE CHILDHOOD – MEMORIAL EDITION
Lenna Bickerton (ISBN 1 901253 13 9) £4.99

"WE'LL GATHER LILACS..."
Lenna Bickerton (ISBN 1 901253 21 X) £5.99

DIESEL TAFF
From 'The Barracks' to Tripoli
Austin Hughes (ISBN 1 901253 14 7) £8.99

A NUN'S GRAVE
A novel set in the Vale Royal of England
Alan K Leicester (ISBN 1 901253 08 2) £7.99

NELLIE'S STORY
A Life of Service
Elizabeth Ellen Osborne (ISBN 1 901253 15 5) £5.99

THE WAY WE WERE
Omnibus edition incorporating Over My Shoulder and Another's War
Les Cooper (ISBN 1 901253 07 4) £7.99

A HOUSE WITH SPIRIT
A Dedication to Marbury Hall
Jackie Hamlett and Christine Hamlett (ISBN 1 901253 19 8) £8.99

WOOLLYBACK
Alan Fleet (ISBN 1 901253 18 X) £8.99

A WHIFF OF FRESH AIR (plus CD)
A collection of humorous Cheshire monologues
Margaret Dignum (ISBN 1 901253 20 1) £9.99

We are always pleased to hear from people who have written accounts of their lives in this area – we believe passionately that their memories should be preserved before it is too late. There has been more change over the last century than at any other time in human history.

From Léonie Press, 13 Vale Rd, Hartford, Northwich, Cheshire CW8 1PL.   Website: www.leoniepress.com